JOHN SOANE

ARCHITECTURAL
Monographs

JOHN SOANE

ACADEMY EDITIONS · LONDON

ST. MARTIN'S PRESS · NEW YORK

Front Cover
Mausoleum of Noel Desenfans, Charlotte (now Hallam) Street, 1807, the prototype of the mausoleum at Dulwich Picture Gallery, 1811. (Dr. xv. 2. 1)

Back Cover
The Dome, 13 Lincoln's Inn Fields, looking east. Drawing by George Bailey, 1810. (Dr. xiv. 6. 3)

Frontispiece
The Pitt cenotaph, National Debt Redemption Office, Old Jewry, 1817. (Dr. xiv. 4. 13)

Title Page
Sir John Soane, RA. Engraving by Charles Turner from the bust by Chantrey, 1831.

Published in Great Britain in 1983 by
ACADEMY EDITIONS
An imprint of the Academy Group Ltd 7 Holland Street London W8 4NA

ISBN 0 85670 830 5 Hardback 0 85670 805 4 Paperback

Published in the United States of America in 1983 by
St. Martin's Press 175 Fifth Avenue New York NY 10010

Library of Congress Catalog Card Number 82-62490
ISBN 0 312 048130 Hardback 0 312 048114 Paperback

Printed and bound in Hong Kong

CONTENTS

Aynho Park, Northamptonshire, design for the vestibule, 1800. Drawing by J. M. Gandy. (Dr. xiii. 4. 4)

Foreword

It is now some 200 years since the inception of Soane's professional career, and we find ourselves today in the midst of a revival of classical theory and practice similar to that to which Soane found himself heir. Hence the sudden renewal of interest in an architect who until comparatively recent years has largely been ignored by the architectural profession, to whom he appeared as being too esoteric, even eccentric, to warrant serious attention. It is to be expected, therefore, that this will bring in its train a corresponding and welcome interest in Soane's critical bibliography, most of which has remained for so long out of print or otherwise unobtainable. It is to fill that gap for the practising architect, student or anyone interested in a general introduction to the work of John Soane that the present *Architectural Monograph* is addressed.

Two essays have been commissioned which identify the main features of Soane's architectural production and locate his work within its historical context. The distinguished architectural historian and Curator of the Soane Museum, Sir John Summerson, in his essay 'Soane: the Man and the Style', identifies the characteristic elements of the Soane style, by looking first at the general picture of the architect's career and, second, at his professional life during its formative years. Summerson draws attention to a number of themes evolved during Soane's creative Middle Period and shows how they were later developed or expanded, concluding with an account of the final years of the architect's life, and his decision to turn his house and its contents into a national institution after his death.

David Watkin's essay is concerned with the similarities—and differences—between Soane's work and that of his contemporaries. The influence of French theory and the French Grand Prix tradition are discussed, and parallels to the work of Soane are evidenced in the work of a number of architects in England and America, as well as in the Franco-Prussian style of around 1800. Watkin also describes the fruitful collaboration between Soane and the painter and personal friend J. M. W. Turner, and quotes from contemporary sources some of the criticism to which the architect was subjected during his lifetime.

The daunting task of approaching the career of so illustrious an architect is made doubly difficult by Soane's prodigious output, numbering some 200 commissions during a long career which embraced such monumental works as the Bank of England. We are extremely fortunate in that of those buildings still remaining, two are of the finest: his own house, now Museum, at Lincoln's Inn Fields, and Dulwich Picture Gallery, both open to the public. Indeed, those who have not experienced the delights of visiting them, so meticulously preserved, are recommended to do so. It is in these two key buildings, both absolutely central to Soane's interests and preoccupations, that the essential qualities of his architecture can be best appreciated. Accordingly, this *Architectural Monograph* focuses on both, and the reader will find, below, an account of the Museum's development written by Sir John Summerson, and illustrated by a number of important plans and sections.

In addition to this 'guided tour' of the development of the Museum, this *Monograph* also takes a privileged look into its archival contents. Contained in the following pages are a number of the highly finished watercolours and drawings which Soane had done especially for the purposes of presenting his buildings, including many which are not on public display. It is worth mentioning that it is to that indefatigable zeal with which Soane acted in his role of self-publicist that we owe this unique privilege today, for although the buildings themselves may be demolished what better way to appreciate their subtleties than in these intense and almost visionary renderings. For this we are indebted to the artists and draughtsmen Soane employed for the purpose at various times, most notably Joseph Michael Gandy.

G.-Tilman Mellinghoff, in his article 'Dulwich Picture Gallery *Revisited*', provides a condensed view of the history of the building and elucidates the complex design process by which Soane created a unique monument for his friend Sir Francis Bourgeois and his enlightened bequest of 360 pictures to the College. Designed by Soane in 1811 when he had reached the height of his creative powers, Dulwich provided him with a challenge in which his friendship with Bourgeois found expression in the ideal rural setting. The result of a slow and painstaking process with several design stages, Dulwich emerged from an unpretentious early design as one of Soane's most individual expressions in architecture, considered by many as the apex of his achievement.

The other key building of Soane's career, the Bank of England, is also treated in a separate survey as seen in some of the watercolours in the Soane Museum and in photographic studies of the building made prior to its demolition in the 1930s.

To complete this *Monograph* a comprehensive list of Soane's built work and a select bibliography are also included.

7

JOHN SUMMERSON

SOANE:

the Man and the Style[1]

JOHN SOANE was the son of a bricklayer of Goring-on-Thames and was born in 1753. At fifteen, determined to be an architect, he entered the service of George Dance. Dance, himself only twenty-seven, had just succeeded his father as clerk-of-the-works to the City of London. He had built only one important building, All Hallows, London Wall, of which more hereafter.

Soane stayed with Dance for about four years. He no doubt attended Thomas Sandby's lectures at the Royal Academy where, in 1772, he obtained the Silver Medal for a measured drawing. Then he went to Henry Holland, another young architect, of a more practical turn than Dance and the son and partner of a successful builder. In 1776, he obtained the Gold Medal of the Royal Academy and, in the following year, was chosen Travelling Student and sent to Italy. He was there for two years and the after-glow of that adventure remained with him all his life. From the Italian journey it is proper to date the beginning of his career as an architect—a career so long and so full that it will be helpful, in due course, to divide it into five sections and look at each separately.

But first, what of Soane, the man? He was tall and thin, with dark hair, a pale, excessively narrow face, bright, nervous eyes and a mouth tightly compressed above the long chin. A somewhat alarming figure, he nevertheless could show himself courteous and gentle, with even a spice of humour. That is how one of his pupils, George Wight-wick, remembered him, but Wightwick also described a darker side: 'an acute sensitiveness, and a fearful irritability, dangerous to himself if not to others; an embittered heart, prompting a cutting and sarcastic mind; uncompromising pride, neither respecting nor desiring respect; a contemptuous regard for the feelings of his dependants; and yet himself the very victim of irrational impulse; with no pity for the trials of his neighbour, and nothing but frantic despair under his own.'[2]

The massive documentation of Soane's life, which he left in his Museum, bears out Wightwick's description. To his friends and intimates he was often a problem. 'I know your constitution', wrote Rowland Burdon, 'it is too eager for stormy weather and easily becomes feverish.'[3] That was written when Soane was fifty-nine, but traces of the same self-torturing temperament are found all along the years. The alienation of his sons, painful episodes with clients, petulant wrangles with his Academy colleagues recur throughout the Soane papers. In his vulnerable singularity he seems actually to have desired to offer to the world something which the world would take amiss. Such offer-ings might possibly be held to include some of his more original architectural adventures.

The Soane style is one of the curiosities of European architecture. In 1792, when it arrives suddenly at maturity, there was not, anywhere in Europe, an architecture as unconstrained by classical loyalties, as free in the handling of proportion and as adventurous in structure and lighting as that which Soane introduced at the Bank of England in that year. How did this style come into being? That we can only answer, in the first place, by looking at the general picture of his career and, in the second, by looking closely at his professional life during those years in which the style emerges. We shall then find two things. We shall find that certain important constituents of the style derive from George Dance.[4] And we shall find that Soane's main contribution was in a novel handling of proportion, a highly personal mode of decorative emphasis and a tendency to arrive at new solutions by the unlimited, often bizarre, distortion of old themes.

Soane's professional career falls, as I have said, into five periods. They are as follows:

1 **Student Period 1776–80** (age 23–27). The main outside influence is French Neoclassicism. The Triumphal Bridge (RA Gold Medal) design derives from an early composition

2 George Dance: All Hallows, London Wall, 1765–67. (Dr. xviii. 7. 7)

3 George Dance: Common Council Chamber, Guildhall, 1777–78.

by Piranesi and from the published designs of M. J. Peyre. In 1778, the year of his departure for Italy, Soane published *Designs in Architecture*, a collection of slight and self-conscious studies for garden buildings in different styles inspired, perhaps, by Chambers' book on the gardens at Kew. During his stay in Italy, 1778–80, he produced several large designs, all influenced by French Neoclassicism. More interesting is the Canine Residence or classical dog-kennel, a *jeu d'esprit* done at the behest of the Bishop of Derry, with 'ancient' and 'modern' versions which foreshadow the duality of style in Soane's later work.

2 **Early Practice Period 1780–91** (age 27–38). The period opened with a bitter disappointment resulting from the casualness of the Bishop of Derry, who had held out in Italy high hopes of patronage which abruptly disappeared at home. Soane had to be content with building small country houses, which he did under the influence of Wyatt and Holland, with occasional immature experimentalism and marked lack of confidence. The publication of these designs in *Plans of Buildings*, 1788, virtually marks the end of this phase and coincides with Soane's appointment as Surveyor to the Bank of England. His country house work, however, continues, with little advance towards maturity, for another three years.

3 **Middle Period 1791–1806** (age 38–53). The happiest and most creative period of Soane's career and the one during which he enjoyed the closest friendship with his mentor, George Dance. A small private income had accrued through the death of his wife's uncle in 1790. Recognition ensued, with official appointments to the Office of Works (1791) and the Office of Woods and Forests (1797) and

election as ARA (1795) and RA (1802). The main elements in the Soane style emerge rapidly in the following works: Wimpole Hall (drawing-room), 1791–93; Bank Stock Office, 1792; his first house in Lincoln's Inn Fields (No. 12), 1792; Buckingham House, 1792–94; Tyringham Hall, 1793–98 (gateway 1794); Rotunda at the Bank, 1796. Soane's 'primitivism', foreshadowed by a dairy design in *Plans of Buildings*, is again evident in the *Sketches in Architecture* of 1793, and is formalized at Bentley Priory (1798) and in the gateway of his country house, Pitzhanger Manor, Ealing (1800–02). During this period Soane started to collect, at Pitzhanger, the material which eventually formed the contents of his Museum.

4 **Picturesque Period 1806–21** (age 53–68). A period of acerbity and trouble in Soane's personal life, beginning with a serious quarrel with Dance, probably in connection with the Professorship of Architecture in the Royal Academy, in which Soane succeeded him. Trouble with his two sons started about 1808 and was followed by Mrs Soane's death, a crushing blow, in 1815. Although there is an almost complete absence of new invention in this period, the contents of the Soane style are recombined and expanded to obtain new and picturesque effects, which Soane called the 'Poetry of Architecture'.[5] The work of preparing the RA lectures widened his horizon. Gothic and Pompeian elements are absorbed into the style and the aesthetic theories of Payne Knight and Uvedale Price were probably influential. Picturesque top-lighting, originated for practical reasons at the Bank, becomes an essential of the style. The Dulwich Picture Gallery, No. 13 Lincoln's Inn Fields (the Soane Museum) and the later Bank halls are

4 A Triumphal Bridge. One of several versions of the design with which Soane won the Gold Medal of the Royal Academy in 1776. (Dr. xii. 5. 2)

the chief works of this period.

5 **Last Period 1821–33** (age 68–80). A lonely period, spent designing large public buildings in the face of much criticism. The Law Courts (begun 1820), Privy Council Offices (1824–27) and Freemasons' Hall (1828) show the ultimate development and expansion of the themes evolved in the Middle Period (1791–1806). In the Royal Palace designs, the King's Robing Room and Royal Gallery of the House of Lords, however, Soane returned to a Neoclassicism which, although mixed with Soanean details, is no advance on his very earliest studies, such as the Triumphal Bridge and the designs done in Italy. To this period belongs the final collecting phase and the crystallization of the Soane Museum as we know it.

Obviously, it is the Middle Period which is the crucial one for the analysis of the Soane style. If we can determine how the Bank Stock Office of 1792 came to assume the form it did, if we can satisfactorily explain that first astonishing manifestation of the style, then our problem is on the way to solution.

First, let us consider the conditions. There are three points to be observed. First, the Bank Stock Office was to be built on the site of the old Office, a site which was confined in such a way that no allowance could be made for any projections to provide additional abutment. Second, whereas the old Office had been timber-roofed, the new building was to be as nearly fire-proof as possible and, therefore, vaulted. Third, the new building was to be top-lit. Baffled by the problem, Soane seems to have consulted

Dance, for the first sketches we have are in his hand.[6] The first study is inspired by the classical type represented by the Basilica of Constantine and the Baths of Diocletian. This type meets the conditions satisfactorily, since the abutment of the main vault is taken into the building, and clerestory lighting is inherent in the cross-section. Such a solution we should expect from any Neoclassically minded architect of the period. Dance's modifications of his chosen model, however, are interesting. Instead of the heavily mullioned windows of the Roman model, he gives us complete glazed semi-circles—a modification which at once recalls a London building of his own designing, the Church of All Hallows, London Wall (fig. 2). This and two other buildings by Dance are so important to our purpose that we must digress to consider them.

All Hallows was Dance's first work, begun in 1765, the year after his return from Rome. It may justly be called the first strictly Neoclassical building in Britain. It is Neoclassical not only in its derivation from a Roman Baths prototype, but more particularly in the treatment of the order which, above cap level, consists of nothing but an enriched architrave. To mutilate the order in this way struck young Soane (Dance's pupil at the time) as wickedly unorthodox. It was his first lesson in shedding the old language and discovering the new.

More important to Soane was a later work by Dance, the Guildhall Common Council Chamber (fig. 3), built in 1777, an innovating design which forestalls much of what we are apt to think of as unique to Soane. The Chamber (de-

11

5, 6 Sketches by George Dance, leading to Soane's design for the Bank Stock Office. (OS. 170, 175)

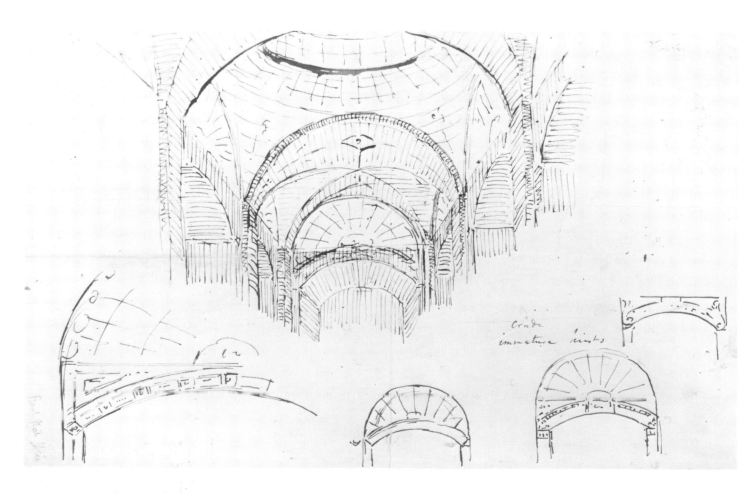

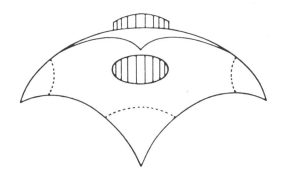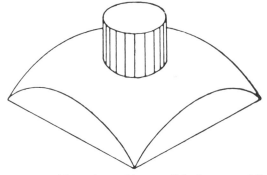

7 Diagram to show 'positive' and 'negative' aspects of the pendentive dome with *oculus* and lantern light (see page 16).

molished in 1906) was a square hall covered by a dome with a central *oculus*. This dome is of a type which had not been seen before in England and not very frequently elsewhere. Its main characteristic is that instead of rising from separate pendentives, as most Byzantine and Renaissance domes do, it is itself a pendentive structure consisting of one continuous spherical surface. There seems to be no conventional description in English for a dome of this kind. In a French treatise on masonry it is called a *cul-de-four en pendentif*[7] and this seems as good a label as any. In our context, *pendentive dome* may be adopted as the appropriate English equivalent.

In the Guildhall example the continuity of surface is not explicit because Dance has introduced decorative 'spandrils', bounded at the top by flattened curves which, with the curves of the four arches, give a 'scalloped' effect like the outer edge of an umbrella. The spandrils do not, in fact, break the surface, which is continuous all the way from the bases of the arches to the *oculus* at the top of the dome.

After Dance's use of the 'pendentive dome' at the Guildhall, it is not found again until Soane takes it up, first in the drawing-room at Wimpole Hall (1791–93), where he repeats Dance's 'scalloped' effect, and then in the Bank Stock Office (1792).

The third Dance building is much closer to the Bank Stock Office in date—in fact contemporary with it—and so close to it in style that we are bound to assume a complete identity of view between the two artists at this date. It must have been about 1792 that Dance was called in by the Marquis of Lansdowne to succeed Robert Adam (who died in that year) at Lansdowne House, to complete the great library, for which Adam had made provision in his plan. Dance's designs for this building are in the Soane Museum. They show a hall covered by a curved (segmental) ceiling, opening, at each end, into a domed space of the Minerva Medica type. Each of these domed spaces is sliced off, vertically, where it meets the hall; and since the domes rise higher than the ceiling between them, there is accommodation in each for a large semi-circular window above ceiling level. These windows light the domed spaces, without being visible from the hall. Now, the design of the junction between hall and domed space is exactly comparable to the alternative version of Dance's first study for the Bank Stock Office, in which there are semi-circular windows over segmental arches.

The next step in the evolution of the Bank Stock Office was the recasting of the centre bay as a domed space, and the continuation of this space in two directions to form, in effect, a 'transept'. The first sketches for this are once again by Dance (figs. 5,6), and the domed space, with its *oculus*, has an obvious affinity with his Guildhall Common Council Chamber. There was, however, another precedent, very near at hand, which from this moment will have affected the issue profoundly. This was the Reduced Annuities Office in the Bank itself (fig. 8), the last building contributed to it by Sir Robert Taylor before his death in 1788.

The Reduced Annuities Office (demolished 1850) was a square hall with segmental wall-arches springing from piers composed of Doric columns. One would expect this arrangement to carry a saucer dome, but instead of a dome there was a circle of windows or, to put it another way, a very large lantern light. We must assume that this mode of top lighting was arrived at empirically, as the solution to a peculiarly difficult problem which the skylights in Taylor's earlier buildings had failed to solve. In any case, Soane chose or was induced to adopt it, and it was to become an important element in the Soane style, and, through Soane, a feature of English architecture of the Regency and beyond.

So the centre bay of the Bank Stock Office became first a domed space with an *oculus* and then a space with pendentives carrying a circular ring of windows and a flattish, conical ceiling. From this point, the elements of the executed design are all present.

The final version of the Bank Stock Office, however, is decidedly different even from the latest preliminary sketches (figs. 9,10). The centre bay has been greatly enlarged and the aisles (what is left of them) pushed into the corners. The end bays have become oblong instead of square and are merely subsidiary extensions of the central space.[8] Nearly all trace of the Roman Baths theme has vanished, and we are presented with a building unclassifiable in terms of any known style. What has happened? It seems that, at some point, Soane decided that a building of this character, subjected to all sorts of practical exigencies, could be liberated completely from classical standards of proportion. The collaboration with Dance, which undoubtedly took place in the earlier stages, carried him some way towards this point, but the last step was taken by Soane himself. Proportion is, in the last resort, a matter of personality, and in Soane the capacity to recognize intuitively an equilibrium of ratios was wayward, or, perhaps one should say, distorted by the psychological tensions which possessed him. Soane held no theories as to proportion.[9] He accepted Laugier's statement that it must necessarily be a question for the individual judgment.[10] The result was that the proportions of his own buildings are subject to no external control. Wherever proportion is not dictated by the modules and intercolumniations of an order, Soane's proportions stray. They stray, it must be confessed, sometimes into that meanness and 'creepiness' which characterize the least lovely of his works. At other times, they are hauntingly memorable.

Few critics would consider the proportions of the Bank Stock Office as 'happy'. They are unclassical—even chaotic. But that is the condition of the building's freedom; and in this uneasy freedom Soane discovered his style. Look now at the ornaments. There is, of course, no classical order; no order could possibly master a composition of such froward and unruly proportions. There is no classical order, but there is a substitute, a token order consisting of vertical strips in relief, in the places where columns or pilasters might be expected to occur. These pilaster-strips play a very important part in the Soane style, and we shall see later that they are symptoms of a 'primitivism' to which Soane subscribed and which will have been connected, in his mind, with the Neoclassical thesis that the bed-rock of architecture is not the canon of the orders but the primitive hut, in which the orders and their parts have their prototypes.

Apart from the pilaster-strips, and the fretted string-course which is a 'token' entablature, the ornament in the Bank Stock Office consists only of delicate plaster panels introduced on the walls and the soffits of the arches, scorings on the spandrils, and *paterae* in appropriate positions. These may perhaps be interpreted as the devices of a classically trained architect to give the composition a sense of punctuation.

When all the elements of the Bank Stock Office have been accounted for and when, in addition, allowance has been made for the fact that the vault is constructed of hollow fire-clay pots necessitating the greatest possible reduction of mass, an inexplicable something—the building's *temperament*—yet remains. That, in any work of art, is the central mystery; it is the mystery of personality, which is also the mystery of style. It can never be wholly isolated and will certainly not be explained until we can explain personality.

The Bank Stock Office is the first building in which the Soane style is completely manifest. The result was obviously arrived at with great difficulty; with some help from Dance in the early stages and painful effort by Soane later on.[11] In a sense, it is the key building of his entire career. Almost all the later examples of the Soane style are related to it in one way or another.

We may now go on to Soane's fourth period, the one I have designated 'Picturesque'. This period starts very approximately in 1806 (when he was fifty-three) and goes on for some fifteen years. I call it 'Picturesque' because I think his work during this period is analogous to that of the landscapists and theoreticians of the Picturesque school. Some remarks in the *Lectures* tend to confirm this and we have, in the Soane Museum, annotated copies of Uvedale Price's and Payne Knight's books[12] which show how closely Soane attended to their ideas. It was in 1806 that Soane was elected Professor of Architecture at the Royal Academy and started on the course of reading and note-taking which equipped him for the lectures he delivered from 1809 onwards. This intensive study greatly widened his horizon and, belatedly, induced him to think of his own style as one uniting the potentialities not only of different kinds of classicism but of Gothic as well. Soane never liked building in Gothic and was clumsy in his few Gothic attempts, but he passionately admired Gothic *effects* and tried to bring them within the capacity of his own style. Gothic effects and Picturesque effects were to him synonymous; they were the 'Poetry of Architecture' which he speaks of in his own description of the breakfast room at the Soane Museum.[13] He identified them, equally, with the effects produced by Vanbrugh, who was his great hero among English architects of the past, the 'Shakespeare of Architects'. So from 1806 we find Soane playing a curious intellectual game with the discoveries he had already made, pulling his pet motifs apart; expanding or compressing them and recombining them in very deliberate attempts to induce the kinds of moods associated with Gothic or with the Picturesque handling of landscape.[14] These attempts were by no means always successful; but they are often profoundly interesting.

One important thing to notice is that after 1806, or indeed, several years before, Soane invented no new themes. All the work after 1806 can be accounted for in terms of the motifs introduced between 1792 and that date. They may be distorted or rearranged in new ways, but they are the old themes, and the old themes alone.

This reinterpretation of thematic material is strikingly illustrated if we pass at once from the Bank Stock Office of 1792 to the Soane Museum dining room of 1812. In this room, Soane introduced a quasi-Gothic element in the hanging arches on the east and west sides. These arches—a wide segmental arch and two semi-circular arches—meet at pendants suggestive of a Gothic vault of the Henry VII type. But if we look closely at their forms, we find that they are also a redistribution of the arch arrangements of the Bank Stock Office. Here is the same combination of segmental and semi-circular arches, while the pendants are pierced transversely by round-headed openings, as are the piers of the Stock Office.

This combination of segmental and semi-circular arches recurs often in Soane's later works. The two shapes do not go comfortably together and we cannot help feeling, sometimes, that their relationship is a piece of deliberate savagery on Soane's part to draw our attention to the way he compensates for the discord by creating dramatic effects of space and light.

One of Soane's most obsessive themes is the 'pendentive

8 Sir Robert Taylor: Reduced Annuities Office, 1782.

9, 10 Bank Stock Office, as completed by Soane in 1792 (*above* Dr. xi. 4.1) and before demolition, c. 1930 (*below*).

11 The Soane family tomb in St Pancras Gardens, London. Built in 1816 in what was then the graveyard of St Giles-in-the-Fields.

dome' rising from these segmental arches. We have already encountered this at the Bank Stock Office. It then recurs in the front parlour of Soane's country house at Ealing, Pitzhanger Manor (1800–02) and again in the breakfast room at the Museum (1812, figs. 1,13). At the Freemasons' Hall in Great Queen Street (1828) something very like the breakfast room dome is snatched out of its context, and made to *hang* from the ceiling over the 'Ark' like a canopy (fig. 12). Here again, as in the Museum dining room, we have the feeling that Soane was trying to produce 'Gothic' effects by the distortion and displacement of classical themes.

Soane's domes are almost invariably designed for interior effect. There is, however, a type of domed surface which is the exact exterior counterpart of these. It is best illustrated in the Soane family tomb in St Pancras Gardens (fig. 11). This extraordinary monument—a metaphor of the temporal within the eternal—consists mainly of a stone *aedicule* of deliberately primitive character, sheltering a marble memorial stone of Ionic delicacy. The monolith which covers the *aedicule* has a domed surface and is surmounted by a cylindrical pinnacle. Now the exterior surface of the dome and pinnacle of the monument correspond with the *interior* surfaces of the breakfast room in the Museum. In other words, a cast taken of the interior of the breakfast room would be, in effect, a model of the exterior of the tomb, that part of the cast formed by the lantern light becoming the 'pinnacle' in the model. The 'pinnacle' apart, the 'positive' version is seen to be very like the lid of an antique cinerary urn of the type which Soane collected and displayed in the library of his Ealing house. The 'positive' thus takes on a funerary character appropriate to the occasion (fig. 7).

In Soane's handling of domes, a variant factor is the size of the *oculus*. In the Bank Stock Office, the opening has been enlarged to the extent that the 'dome' has come to consist merely of confluent pendentives supporting the circular lantern. In two of the later Bank halls, however—the Colonial Office and the Old Dividend Office—this arrangement is modified in a spectacular way. A true pendentive dome springs at some ten feet from the floor and rises without interruption, on semi-circular arches, so that the impression of a domed interior is preserved and the opening to the lantern can be read as a large *oculus*. Soane's most intrepid expansion of the *oculus* is seen in the design of the Court of Chancery at Westminster (fig. 19). In this, one of Soane's very last works, the expansion of an old theme is stretched just as far as it will go. The arches of the dome are drawn out to an exceedingly flat five-centred curve, while the *oculus* is so large as to dispose of all the dome except the confluent spandrils which become little more than the shaped soffit of a circular cantilevered gallery. The arches hanging from the ceiling are related to the hanging arches in the Museum dining room. The interior as a whole is the most dramatic and surprising of Soane's conversions of the themes of the 1790s. It underlines again his inability to invent new themes after a certain date and his reliance on those which had become an integral part of his stock of ideas in the period when Dance was so often at his elbow.

I mentioned earlier the 'primitivist' element which is so important a factor in the Soane style and makes its first appearance in a design for a dairy (fig. 14), given in his *Plans of Buildings* of 1788. Then, in the *Sketches in Architecture*, published in 1793, are a number of designs for cottages, some of which have loggias or porches, built of

12 Freemasons' Hall, Great Queen Street, London. Built in 1828–30. (N. Drg. Rm.)

13 Pitzhanger Manor, Ealing, built in 1800–02. The front parlour. (Pic. Rm.)

14 Dairy at Hammels Park, Hertfordshire, 1783. (Dr. xiii. 7. 1)

rustic-work, or, as Soane describes one of them, 'trunks of trees decorated with woodbines and honeysuckles'. This 'natural' architecture was already in vogue; there are earlier specimens among the Adam designs in the Soane Museum, and it is related not to any real vernacular practice, but to the primitive hut mentioned by Vitruvius and construed by later writers as the prototype of all architectural forms. Laugier lays particular stress on the hut as the fundamental embodiment of architectural principles and in the English translation of his *Essai* of 1755 is a charming frontispiece showing the hut in process of erection by a team of savages. Sir William Chambers, in his *Treatise* of 1759, illustrates it most precisely.

In Soane's pair of cottages of 1793, the primitive order is shown with the bark still on the trunks, but cut away at the caps under the square abacus, giving a retracted necking. This form Soane proceeded, a few years later, to translate into other materials—first into flint, then into brick, with successive refinements of detail. A design for a park entrance of about 1796 (fig. 15) shows flint pilasters and a primitive 'entablature' with brick 'triglyphs' under the eaves. In the gateway (c. 1801) at Pitzhanger Manor, the piers consist of coupled flint pilasters with a retracted 'frieze' over each pair and, above that, a capping which is

an antique sarcophagus lid.

The 'primitivist' style reaches its full development in one of Soane's most individual buildings, the Dulwich Picture Gallery of 1811–14. Here was a case where a building of dignified character was required, but where the funds were extremely limited. The site was in a country setting and Soane at this period was under the spell of the Picturesque; so it was natural that he should bring his primitivist order into play. It is in stock brick, with a retracted stone frieze and a rudimentary stone cornice. It finds expression in the wings of the building and again in the founder's mausoleum (fig. 16), and is used much as one of the Palladian orders might be used, but with a greater freedom of proportion, and a very striking freedom of composition.

The Dulwich building was originally meant to consist of a picture gallery with a mausoleum attached. Then it was decided to incorporate apartments for six almswomen who were dependent on the collegiate foundation. A gallery, a mausoleum and a set of almhouses may seem to offer a somewhat unpromising combination for successful architectural treatment but Soane, by adroit articulation of the three elements, arrived at a result of wonderful vitality, a result which reminds one a little of the way Vanbrugh, on a

18

15 Design for a gateway and lodges at Bagshot Park, Surrey, c. 1796. (Pic. Rm.)

very different scale, articulated the parts of his great houses. Dulwich has 'the variety in heights as well as in projections' which Soane stressed as one of Vanbrugh's great merits.

The attached mausoleum developed in a curious way. The interior arrangement, consisting of a circular Greek Doric vestibule abruptly joined to a tomb-cell, brilliantly lit through an opening in its domical ceiling, was worked out in 1808 for Bourgeois' private mausoleum in Charlotte Street, Portland Place (now Hallam Street, just behind the RIBA). There, it was squeezed into a back garden and had, to all intents and purposes, no exterior. Transferred to Dulwich, the question of its exterior expression at once arose. Soane took a hint here from Robert Adam's remarkable church at Mistley with its twin towers. Finally, at Dulwich, there is the lantern over the mausoleum, a little cage of light, whose tensions are emphasized by thin incised lines in the masonry, a feature for which Soane is always remembered and sometimes mocked. Here they seem wonderfully eloquent.

From Dulwich, which may be seen as the quintessence of the Soane style, we must return again to the 1790s and examine yet another Dance-Soane theme, this time the cross-vault ceiling. In Soane's work it first appears in the ground-floor back parlour of his first London house, No. 12 Lincoln's Inn Fields built in 1792, but Dance seems to have used something very like it at Cranbury Park, Hants., c.1780, while the pattern was used as a flat ceiling design in the 'Alambra' at Kew, built in 1756 and engraved in Chambers' *Treatise*. The prototype of the whole series is, no doubt, an engraving by Santo Bartoli[15] of the ceiling of one of the Etruscan tombs at Corneto.

The geometry of this type of ceiling is complicated. The ceiling may be described as a cross-vault whose interpenetrations have been cut back to produce triangular 'chamfers' broadening upwards to the apex of the ceiling where they meet as four sides of a square. Dance perhaps, and Soane certainly, saw in this pattern a touch of Gothic romance, the flying lines from the corners to the centre giving a faint idea of a ribbed vault. In Soane's work it begins as a flat pattern on a low domical ceiling, but later is articulated as a cross-vault with double groins. As such it appears in the Pitt Cenotaph at the National Debt Redemption Office (1818–19). But it makes its most volatile appearance in the Privy Council Chamber of 1824. Here, it is introduced as a sort of canopy, with daylight filtering in at the edges. This is the same daylighting device which Soane

16 Dulwich Picture Gallery, the lantern over the founder's mausoleum, 1811–12.   17 The library, 13 Lincoln's Inn Fields, 1812.

used first in the Soane Museum breakfast room of 1812, but it goes back to the indirect lighting of the *exedrae* in Dance's Lansdowne House design. Possibly it originated in the 'lumière mystérieuse' of certain French churches which Soane mentions approvingly in his lectures.[16]

I have drawn attention to five separate themes belonging to Soane's creative Middle Period and shown how he developed or expanded them in his later Picturesque Period. The style was evolved rapidly and completely within a few years when Soane was aged, say, between thirty-eight and forty-five and when he had the advantage of frequent discussion with and help from George Dance. Everything before that period was more or less derivative; everything afterwards depended on the half-dozen or so themes of the creative period. These were combined, expanded, converted, inverted and modified in all sorts of ways, but not a single new theme was added to their number. Soane became the prisoner of his own style.

Of the extent of Soane's debt to George Dance enough has been said, but in the case of a Soane building of the 1790s, previously mentioned, the Rotunda at the Bank of England (1796), we have documentary proof of it; for Soane

preserved some little scribbles of a domed interior clearly related to the Rotunda, on one of which he wrote 'Sketch by Mr G. Dance'. I am not suggesting that any of Soane's architecture is George Dance *sous clef*. It is not; it is something quite different, with the unmistakable Soane temperament. Indeed, the master may, in his later work, have owed something to the pupil, for in a letter of 1802 he writes: 'You wou'd do me a great favour and a great service, if you wou'd let me look at your plan of Mr Praed's house, I want to steal from it.'[17]

What is beyond doubt, however, is that the style which we all know as the Soane style is the work not of one man but of two. Sir John Soane would not have denied this for a moment, for in his lifetime he never ceased, even during their estrangement, to acknowledge his indebtedness to his 'revered master'. There stands today, in the Soane Museum, the great chest which Sir John designed to enclose his collection of George Dance's drawings. It is sometimes observed that it looks like a sarcophagus. It is also very like a shrine.

Soane formally retired from practice in 1833, when he was eighty. In the same year, he obtained the private Act of

18 Pitzhanger Manor, Ealing, the library. (Pic. Rm.)

Parliament under which his house and its contents were to become a national institution after his death. The decision so to dispose of his house—and of his fortune in endowing it—meant the end of a dream; the dream which had inspired the building of Pitzhanger more than thirty years before, the dream that he would be succeeded by architect sons and be, in fact, the founder of a line of architects who, benefiting from the lessons of his own career, would march from triumph to triumph in the exposition of their art. To this dynastic ideal he had applied every conceivable endeavour and by his very earnestness had driven his sons to revolt against it. Pitzhanger, built while they were still boys, was planned as the ideal environment for a classic breed of architects, and it was there and for that purpose that the idea of a Soane *Museum*—the word still had a Parnassian ring—came into being. In 1810, however, Pitzhanger was given up. John, the eldest son, had shown little liking for architecture and had got himself engaged. George wanted to write plays. Both John and George married in 1811, both unsuitably and George, on his own admission, out of sheer spite towards his parents. Between him and his father a terrible feud began, which ended only with the father's death.

It was under the lowering shadow of these troubles that Soane had undertaken, in 1812, the rebuilding of No. 13 Lincoln's Inn Fields. An index to his state of mind at that time is provided by a draft, in his own hand, of an article imagined to be by an antiquary of the future, who speculates on the origin of the building and concludes it to have been the residence of a great architect who suffered for his originality and integrity, was abused even by his own kin, and died of a broken heart. Notwithstanding these forebodings, the new house was equipped to receive all the treasures of Pitzhanger, while, year after year, more treasures were added. Mrs Soane died in 1815; John Soane, the elder and less hostile son, in 1823; while George, by this time a grimly unsuccessful novelist, sank into a hopeless condition of Bohemianism and embitterment. But the Museum increased. Hogarth's *Election* pictures were added in 1823. The picture room and monk's parlour were built and, in 1824, the great Belzoni sarcophagus arrived. Every year antiquities and curiosities were bought or paintings commissioned. In 1830 Soane himself, with an intuition of finality, wrote his first *Description* of the building and its contents and circulated it to his friends. The decision of 1833 must gradually have been borne in upon him as the only possible way of salvaging this hoarded cargo from the shipwrecked dream. If no dynasty of artists should succeed him, at least the Museum, its intended nursery and dowry, should stand as his memorial, and serve the profession which he had loved with such ferocious passion.

19 The Court of Chancery, Westminster, built in 1822–25, demolished 1883. (Dr. xvi. 1. 2)

NOTES

1 This essay is a revised and condensed version of the text of the author's, *Sir John Soane*, London 1952.

2 Wightwick's autobiography was published in detached papers in *Bentley's Miscellany*, 1852. The passages relating to Soane are reprinted in A. T. Bolton, *The Portrait of Sir John Soane, R.A.*, 1927, pp. 395–410.

3 Bolton, *ibid.*, p. 179.

4 For the life and work of Dance, see D. Stroud, *George Dance, Architect, 1741–1825*, 1971.

5 J. Soane, *Lectures on Architecture*, ed. A. T. Bolton, 1929, p. 53.

6 These and other early sketches for the Stock Office are pasted into an album entitled on the spine, *Original Sketches: Miscellaneous Architectural Subjects Chiefly by Sir J. Soane* (Soane Case, shelf C).

7 J.B. De La Rue, *Traité de la Coupe des Pierres*, Paris 1728, pp. 62–63.

8 H. R. Steele and F. R. Yerbury, *The Old Bank of England*, 1930, pp. 10 and 27.

9 J. Soane, *Lectures, op. cit.*, p. 100, where he condemns theories of proportion as 'neither applicable nor useful'.

10 M. A. Laugier, *Essai sur l'architecture*, 1753, p. 121. 'There is nothing but the natural taste joined to great practice, which assuredly guide the architects in this dark road'.

11 Soane was acutely conscious of his own difficulties. 'Architecture is an Art purely of Invention (as opposed to Imitation in painting and sculpture), and Invention is the most painful and the most difficult exercise of the human mind.' (*Lectures, op. cit.*, p. 119). This is one of the few passages in Soane's writings which seem to allude to the originality of his own work. He never, as Robert Adam did, described or analysed his own style.

12 U. Price, *Essay on the Picturesque*, 1794, and R. Payne Knight, *An Analytical Enquiry into the Principles of Taste*, 1805.

13 *Description of the House and Museum*, etc., 1832, p. 54.

14 'Why should we not unite the variety of figure, the wild effects, the bold combinations of cultivated Art, with all the regularity displayed in the Ancient Architecture?' (*Lectures, op. cit.*, p. 157.)

15 *Gli Antichi Sepolcri trovati in Roma*, 1768.

16 'The *lumière mystérieuse*, so successfully practised by the French artist, is a most powerful agent in the hands of a man of genius, and its power cannot be too fully understood, nor too highly appreciated. It is, however, little attended to in our Architecture, and for this obvious reason, that we do not sufficiently feel the importance of Character in our buildings.' (*Lectures*, p. 126.)

17 A.T. Bolton, *The Portrait of Sir John Soane, op. cit.*, pp. 94–95.

The Soane Museum
13 Lincoln's Inn Fields

Soane's building works in Lincoln's Inn Fields developed in four stages through a period of forty years. First, in 1792, when he was thirty-nine, he built No. 12 as a family house, with his professional office on the site of the stables at the back. Second, in 1808, he bought the larger house next door, No. 13. He did not at once rebuild this but pulled down the stables and replaced them with an eastward extension of his office behind No. 12. This extension comprised the present 'Dome' and a new two-storey office beyond, and gave the opportunity for a three-fold facade facing the narrow street called Whetstone Park (see drawing below). This facade, which is still intact, was the first piece of Soane's exterior architecture consciously to express the character of a museum.

The third stage was the building of the main house, No. 13, in 1812, as a residence, with a triple loggia (which Soane called the 'verandah') of Portland stone towards the street. The fourth and last stage belongs to 1824, when Soane was seventy-one. This consisted in the acquisition and demolition of No. 14 and its subsequent rebuilding in two parts— at the back as an extension of the 'museum', consisting of the picture room and monk's parlour, and in front as a terrace house with a facade exactly matching that of No. 12. Soane eventually sold the house, keeping only the buildings and courtyard behind it.

By 1825 (the date of the plans on the following page) Soane had let No. 12 (including his old office) on long lease, and sold No. 14, thus establishing the limits of the 'House and Museum of Sir John Soane' to which the Act of 1833 was to give statutory protection. In 1869, however, the Trustees reclaimed the old office from No. 12 and incorporated the space in the Museum. Exactly a hundred years later, in 1969, the Trustees re-occupied the whole of No. 12 and connected it, at three levels, with No. 13, to form an integral part of the Museum.

Sir John Summerson

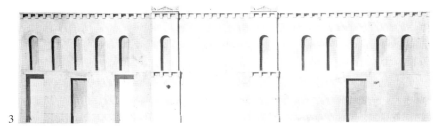

1 No. 13 Lincoln's Inn Fields. As originally built in 1812, the Portland stone 'verandah' was unglazed and the building rose only to the main cornice level. 'Attic storeys' were added to all three houses in 1832.

2 Nos 12, 13 and 14 Lincoln's Inn Fields, built by Soane in 1792, 1812 and 1824 respectively. Drawing by Alison Shepherd, 1954.

3 The rear elevation to Whetstone Park, built in 1809 and articulating the three elements in Soane's building work of that year. *Centre:* the 'Plaister Room' (now the 'Dome'). *Right:* Soane's old office, remodelled as a library. *Left:* new office at two levels. Of the four doorways, two (tinted dark) are dummies; the other two led originally into an inner court and the lower office respectively. (Dr. xxxii. 3. 43)

4 The Breakfast Room, No. 12 Lincoln's Inn Fields. Built in 1792 as the ground-floor back of No. 12, the room contains the earliest of Soane's splayed cross-vault ceilings. The painted decorations are probably by John Crace. The foliage seen through the window belongs to potted plants on the roof of Soane's office, later converted into a library. Drawing by J. M. Gandy, c. 1794. (Dr. xiv. 6. 1)

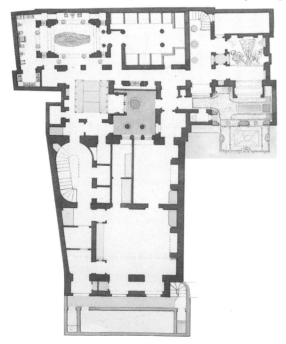

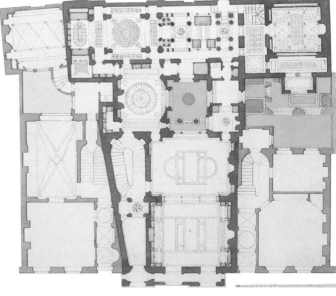

5,6 Plans of Nos 12, 13 and 14 Lincoln's Inn Fields, drawn by C. J. Richardson, 1825. *Left*: basement of No 13. *Right*: ground floors of Nos 12, 13 and 14. (SD 1,2)

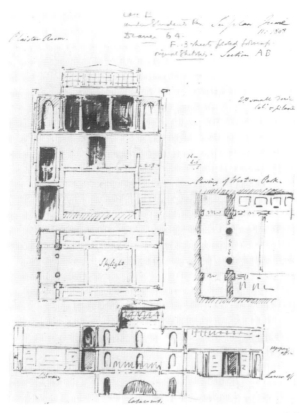

7 Soane's first sketches for the rear extension of No. 12 Lincoln's Inn Fields, June 1808. The new building was to consist of the old office recon-structed as a library; a 'Plaister Room', for display of casts, with 'Cata-combs' below; an 'Upper Office' and 'Lower Office'. (Dr. xxxii. 2A(c))

8 The Lower Office, formed in 1808, partly in an existing structure and decorated with re-used woodwork and plaster casts. This was destroyed in 1821 when Soane altered the floor levels and formed the Colonnade and Students' Room, again re-using old materials. Drawing by Soane's pupil, J. Adams, showing the door and window to the inner court. (PSA 33)

9

10

11

9, 10, 11 Views at different levels of Soane's first design for the Plaister Room and Catacombs, June 1808. The design contains the idea of a perforated floor so that while the upper room, with its display of casts, is strongly lit, the more funereal exhibits in the basement are in a subdued light. Drawings by J. Adams, June 1805. (PSA 34, 37, 35)

12, 13 In Soane's second design for the Plaister Room, the floor has two perforations with a 'gangway' between them. The roof light has been enlarged into a lantern containing four lunettes and supported, in one version, by iron columns. (PSA 31, 30)

14 Soane's third design disposes of the intermediate floor altogether so that the chamber rises without interruption from basement to roof light, the latter now supported on pendentives. The design led immediately to the executed version, illustrated on the following pages. From being conceived as the 'Plaister Room' this space became the 'Museum' and today is called the 'Dome'. (PSA 36)

George Bailey

15

16

17

16 The Dome in 1813. A study by Joseph Michael Gandy, illustrating the 'lumière mystérieuse' which so strongly appealed to Soane. The space is lit partly by daylight from the lantern over the dome and partly by a lamp hidden behind a projecting fragment of cornice. (Office)

17 Another view by J. M. Gandy, 1813. Here the Dome is seen at night, dramatically lit from a source in the crypt. The play of shadow, however, owes something to Gandy's imagination. (Dr. xiv. 6. 5)

18

15 The Dome in 1810. Section looking east, drawn by Soane's chief clerk, George Bailey. The exhibits above ground-floor level are almost all plaster casts and include the huge cornice and architrave of Castor and Pollux, wedged into the upper arch. The capital from the same order is against the wall in the passage on the right. The miniature plan (*bottom right*) shows that at this date Soane considered remodelling No. 12 and using the whole site of No. 13 as a Museum and Gallery. (Dr. xiv. 6. 3)

18 The Dome, after the Belzoni Sarcophagus had been added to the collection in 1824. Drawing by C. J. Richardson. (SD 47)

19 Detail of the east respond of the arches separating the Library from the Dining Room. The four slim pillars are of metal; the arched superstructure is a mixture of wood and plaster, the pedestal and book-cases are in mahogany and the walls are painted a Pompeian red. The convex mirror on the left and the flush mirror in the recess on the right contribute to the sense of transparency and penetration in the architecture of these rooms.

20 The Dining Room seen from the Library. The dividing screen originally consisted of a trio of semi-circular hanging arches (see the views on page 39) but Soane eventually cut away the central arch, perhaps to afford better views of the paintings by Henry Howard which were installed in the ceilings of the two rooms in 1832.

21 The Dome, looking east, with Chantrey's bust of Soane (1830) centred on the balustrade.

22 A view in the Monk's Parlour showing the junction of the three spaces of which this part of the building consists (compare the sections, page 36).

23

24

23 Section through the Dome and the Breakfast Room, looking east. The Dome, with its stone-coloured walls is part of the Museum; the Breakfast Room, finished throughout in oak graining, is part of the House. Glazed doors connect the two scenes. On the Breakfast Room walls are engravings of Roman mural decorations (from the Villa Negroni) which were among Soane's sources of inspiration. Through the window is the Monument Court with the Dressing Room window beyond. Drawn by F. Copland, 1817. (PSA 1)

24 Plan and section of the Breakfast Room. The shallow pendentive dome, detached from the walls at either end, gives the effect of a canopy. The ornaments are sunk or incised to preserve the primitive geometry of the room. (SD 24)

25 Soane's own description of the Breakfast Room concludes as follows: 'The views from this room into the Monument Court and into the Museum, the mirrors in the ceiling, and the looking-glasses, combined with the variety of outline and general arrangement and the design and decoration of this limited space, present a succession of those fanciful effects which constitute the poetry of architecture.'

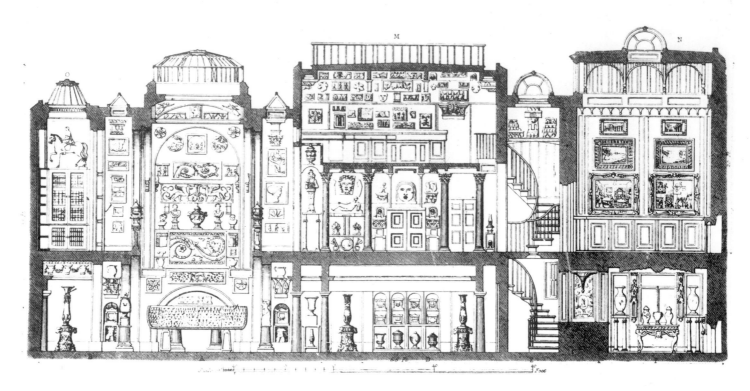

26 Section from west to east through the Dome, Colonnade and Picture Room. The central element is a partial rebuilding of Soane's Upper and Lower Offices of 1809 after he had altered the floor levels in 1821. The Upper Office has become the present Students' Room, supported independently on Corinthian columns. From this brilliantly lit room, light filters down to the ground floor, and, on the north, still further down to the otherwise completely obscure Crypt, as shown in the cross-section below.

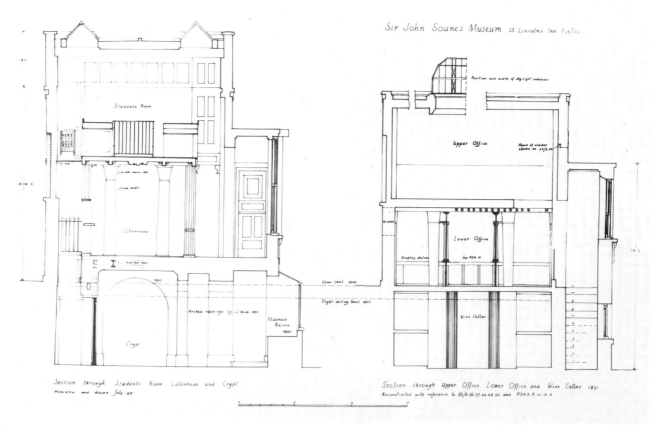

27 Sections from north to south, through the Students' Room, Colonnade and Crypt. The diagram on the left shows the building as existing, including alterations made in 1890, which admit more light into the Crypt than Soane intended. That on the right is a reconstruction of the building before 1821. Drawing by John Summerson, 1981.

36

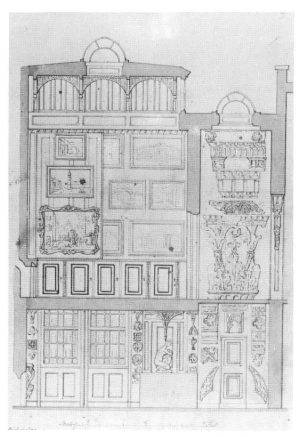

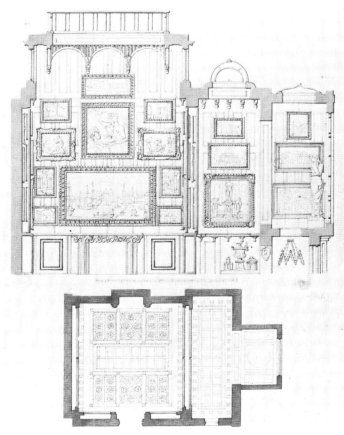

28, 29 The Picture Room and Monk's Parlour, added to the Museum in 1824. *Left:* section, looking south, through the Picture Room and Corridor, with the Monk's Parlour below. *Right:* section looking east, through the Picture Room and the Recess which connects vertically with the Monk's Parlour and horizontally with the Picture Room through two pairs of hinged planes, carrying framed paintings on both sides. Another pair of planes is hinged to the opposite wall. The plan shows a reflection of the Picture Room ceiling. (SD 80, 82)

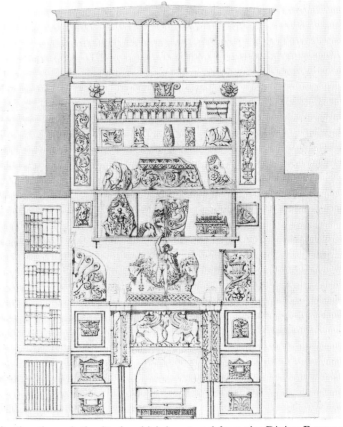

30 Section looking east through the Corridor, adjoining the Picture Room and showing the stairs to the Students' Room and the Crypt. The casts of the Castor and Pollux order, which formed a conspicuous feature of the Dome were brought here in 1824. The cap and cornice are seen here in profile. The section, top left, shows them in elevation. (SD 77)

31 Section through the Study which is entered from the Dining Room at its north-east corner. Here Soane arranged the architectural fragments collected in Rome by C. H. Tatham. The roof is top-lit but also has a large window looking into the Monument Court. (SD 17)

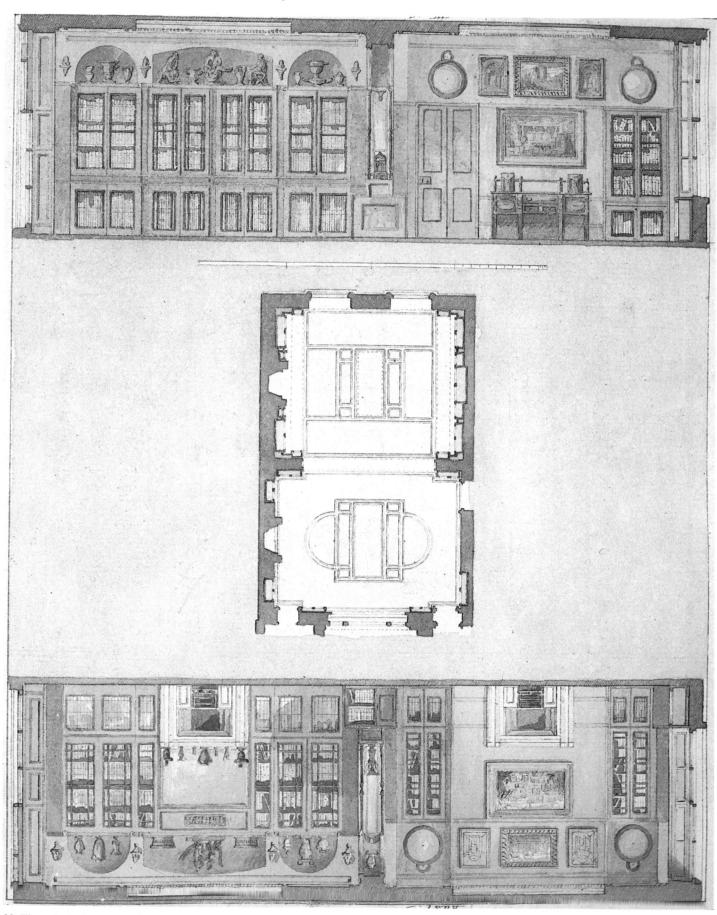

32 The principal rooms on the ground floor of No. 13 Lincoln's Inn Fields. Plan of the Dining Room and Library with elevations of the west and east walls. (SD 5)

33, 34 Views of the Dining Room and Library, drawn by C. J. Richardson in 1825. *Above:* the Library looking north-east into the Dining Room. *Below:* the Dining Room, looking south-west. In this view the Cawdar vase (4th century B.C.) stands between the windows. On the far right is a model of the Soane family tomb. (SD 8, 9)

DAVID WATKIN

SOANE

and his Contemporaries

JOHN SOANE confronts us with the paradox of a dedicated upholder of the classical tradition in architecture who was at the same time a romantic artist following a lonely path in an idiosyncratic style far removed from that practised by his contemporaries. No English architect was more given to devising megalomaniac public buildings in the French Grand Prix manner,[1] yet none achieved a more personal and imaginative individual style. Soane's work derives much of its visual and intellectual piquancy from this fruitful tension between public doctrine and private practice. Moreover, to study Soane is to be faced with the problem of the expression of personality in architecture, for it is surely possible to find in his work reflections of the edginess and vanity, the persecution complex and the unyielding Old Testament morality, the inner conflicts, uncertainties and introspection which we know were fundamental to his character. If the prime purpose of the present paper is to relate Soane to his contemporaries, then it is arguable that the most interesting and fundamental way in which he differs from them is that the intransigent strangeness of his work forces us to consider how far the mystery of personality can be expressed in architecture. Ever conscious of his humble origins, he was ruthlessly ambitious as is clear, for example, from the long list of publications which he devoted to promoting his own work. On the whole, people receive the treatment not that they deserve but that they expect; and Soane certainly expected the hostility which was frequently directed to him both as a man and as an architect. He comforted himself with the thought that most great architects, as he put it in a letter of 1807, have suffered 'a life of difficulty and distress, of neglect and contempt'.[2]

When we speak of the Neoclassical movement in eighteenth-century England, it could be claimed that we are describing simply a late stage in the acclimatization of this country to the all'antica ideals of the Italian Renaissance. A study tour in Italy itself was always an essential part of this process. The impressive list of architects who underwent this formative experience includes William Chambers (born 1723), in Paris and Italy 1749–55; Robert Adam (born 1728), in Italy 1754–58; Robert Mylne (born 1734) in Paris and Italy 1754–58; George Dance (born 1741), in Rome 1758–65; Thomas Harrison (born 1744), in Rome 1769–76; James Wyatt (born 1747), in Venice and Rome 1762–68; James Lewis (born c. 1751), in Rome 1770–72; Thomas Hardwick (born 1752), in Rome with Soane 1776–79;[3] and John Soane (born 1753), in Rome 1778–80. In 1776 Soane had won the Royal Academy Gold Medal with his Triumphal Bridge design and was accordingly fortunate enough to be selected by George III for the award of a three-year Travelling Studentship. The circumstances of his arrival in Italy were thus an amateurish English echo of those by which the highly trained products of the French Academy were dispatched as pensionnaires to the French Academy in Rome.

Although Soane arrived in Rome over twenty years after Adam, he still studied the same range of monuments from Hadrian's Villa to the Villa Madama. These Italian study tours also involved the familiarizing of English architects with the approach to design of the French Grand Prix winners (figs. 1,2). Their vast paper projects for public buildings inspired by the Baths of ancient Rome, the Pantheon and the imperial villas, were designed axially, symmetrically and with no consideration whatsoever for their relation to any real or even imaginary site. They were thus markedly lacking in potential application within the more empirical context of English architectural practice. Nonetheless, during his time in Rome Soane designed in this manner a British Senate House, a Royal Palace, a Monument to the Earl of Chatham, a Canine Residence, a Castello d'Acqua which he entered for the competition at Parma in 1780, and a variant of his Triumphal Bridge design of 1776 inspired by the Greek Doric he had seen at Paestum in December 1778.[4] The bridge is among the

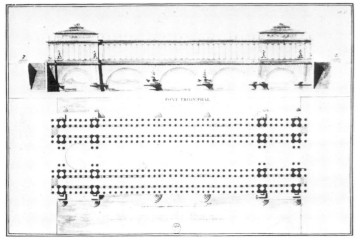

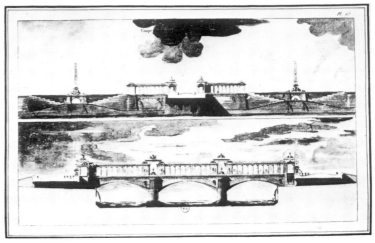

1 French Academy Grand Prix design for a Triumphal Bridge by Lefebure, 1783.

2 French Academy Grand Prix design for a Triumphal Bridge by Wagniat, 1786.

building types which are least appropriate as occasions for elaborate architectural display. Soane could, however, point as sources to fanciful bridge designs by Palladio, by Piranesi in c.1750 and by Sandby in 1760. The megalomaniac scale and vast quadrant colonnades of Soane's project are, of course, derived from Grand Prix projects as exemplified in the pages of M.J. Peyre's influential *Oeuvres d'architecture* of 1765 (figs. 3,4). Soane was not alone in devoting his time in Rome to such visionary Neoclassical schemes:[5] Chambers had designed a mausoleum for the Prince of Wales in 1751; Mylne had won a silver medal in the Concorso Clementino at the Accademia di San Luca in 1758 with his design for a 'Public Building with Memorial Gallery to exhibit busts of eminent men';[6] James Byres won a prize in the same Concorso in 1762 with a design for a palace; Dance had won the Parma Gold Medal in 1763 with his design for a 'Public Gallery for Statues, Pictures, etc.'; and Harrison entered the Concorso Balestra in 1773 with a project for the Piazza del Popolo in Rome. Thus at this stage in his career—and by 1780 he was already twenty-seven—Soane's interests are characteristic of those of the most stylistically advanced architects of the day. One of the aspects of his career which subsequently set him apart from those architects was his continuing preoccupation with such stylophilistic fantasies. Amongst the curiosities of his style which may be related to some inner vanity is that once he had got hold of an idea he did not develop it but repeated it again and again. He could not bear to drop his youthful project for a Triumphal Bridge but toyed with it over the years, exhibiting versions of it at the Royal Academy in 1799 and 1806; six framed drawings relating to it hang in the Soane Museum and many others are stored in drawers. Similarly, his designs of the 1770s for palaces recur in his work as late as the 1820s and 1830s. One of these boasts a spectacular Pantheon dome sheltering an inner dome which Soane claimed would allow light to percolate mysteriously into the great hall below. In describing this effect in 1828 as 'lumière mystérieuse',[7] a phrase he also used in his Royal Academy lectures from 1809, Soane made clear his debt to romantics within the French classical tradition like Le Camus de Mézières and Boullée. In his influential book, *Le génie de l'architecture, ou l'analogie de cet art avec nos sensations* (1780), Le Camus had adumbrated a Picturesque theory intended to undermine the traditional Cartesian certainties of French rationalism. For him, light could make architecture 'mystérieuse ou triste'. Boullée elaborated these hints in his own bizarre theories and designs, writing in c.1790 in his *Architecture, Essai sur l'art*, that 'C'est la lumière qui produit les effets. . . Si je peu éviter que la lumière arrive directement, et la faire pénétrer sans que le spectateur aperçoive d'où elle part, les effets résultans d'un jour mystérieux produiront des effets inconcevables . . .'.[8] Boullée's *Essai* was not published until 1953, but clearly Soane was familiar with the lessons which Boullée taught his many pupils. It has recently been suggested[9] that the two men may have met in Paris in 1778 and that Soane knew of Boullée's scheme for covering the Madeleine with a twin-shelled dome (fig. 5). Furthermore, the inner dome of Soane's palace was to have been adorned with a machinery reproducing the effect of the solar system in a manner reminiscent of Boullée's celebrated Cenotaph to Newton. Also from France came language such as the 'Poetry of Architecture'[10] which Soane used in 1835 to describe the effects of his breakfast room at Lincoln's Inn Fields. In his *Essai* Boullée had written that 'Nos édifices, surtout les édifices publics, devroient être, en quelque façon, des poèmes.'[11] It was, of course, from the English tradition of the Picturesque as encapsulated in the writings of Price and Knight in the 1790s, that Soane derived his sensitivity to the kind of variety and intricacy, concealment and exposure, light and shade, that characterized the spatial organization of the Soane Museum. However, in his determination to achieve singularity he justified that planning not by English but by French analogies.

Soane's devotion to the theories of the Abbé Laugier is well known, thanks perhaps to the bizarre circumstance of his possessing as many as eleven copies of the *Essai sur l'architecture* (1753). It is not necessary to rehearse here Laugier's reductionist doctrine, derived from Frémin and Cordemoy, which proposed that the elements of the orders ought always to be load-bearing and that inert masses such as the wall should be eliminated as far as possible. It should not be supposed that Soane's admiration for Laugier was unusual. In his *Complete Body of Architecture* (1756), even a leading second-generation Palladian like Isaac Ware could swallow the gospel according to Laugier without apparently realizing that if put into practice it would

3 M. J. Peyre: Project for the Hôtel de Condé, c. 1765.

4 J. Soane: Design for a Royal Palace, 1821, 1831. (Pic. Rm.)

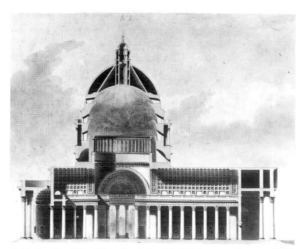

5 E. L. Boullée: Church of the Madeleine, section, c. 1777.

6 J. Soane: Chillington Hall, Staffordshire, 1785–89.

7 H. Emlyn: Beaumont Lodge, Berkshire, c. 1790.

completely undermine the kind of architecture which he and his clients wanted to put up. Ware follows Frémin and Laugier by stripping classical architecture of all ornament in his search for naturalness and authenticity. He attacks not only the pilaster, since it is manifestly non load-bearing, but also pedestals below columns, fluting on columns and even columns with entasis: the reason being that such ornament conflicts with the *reality* of a column which is supposed to be the representation of the trunk of a tree. This is analagous to the argument proposed by both Cordemoy and Laugier that one should not place statues on the skyline of buildings because it would not be natural for humans to stand there. 'There is a nobleness in simplicity', Ware argued, 'which is always broken in upon by ornament: therefore no ornament should be admitted but what is reasonable; and nothing is reasonable in architecture which is not founded on some principle of use.'[12]

It is language of this kind, derived from Laugier and Ware, that Soane used in support of his own work in the Introduction to his *Plans, Elevations and Sections of Buildings erected in the Counties of Norfolk, Suffolk*, etc., which he published in 1788 at the age of thirty-five: 'Ornaments are to be cautiously introduced; those ought only to be used that are simple, applicable and characteristic of their situations; they must be designed with regularity and be perfectly distinct in their outlines; the Doric

members must not be mixed with the Ionic, nor the Ionic with the Corinthian, but such ornaments should only be used, as tend to show the destination of the edifice, as assist in determining its character, and for the choice of which the architect can assign satisfactory reasons.'[13]

The buildings by Soane which he selected for illustration, such as Shotesham Park, Letton Hall, Chillington Hall, Tendring Hall and Ryston Hall, are typical of the best of English architecture in the 1780s: that is to say they are simply elegant variants on the Palladianism of men like Paine and Ware enlivened with a new tautness inspired by the reductionist doctrines of Laugier. At this stage in his career, Soane's work is virtually indistinguishable from that of his contemporaries like Mylne or Johnson. The change came when in 1785–89 he built the hall at Chillington (fig. 6) in a different style from that shown in his published designs of 1788, and in 1792 when he designed the Bank Stock Office. Sir John Summerson's beautiful description of the emergence, in 1792, of Soane's abstract inward-looking style need not be repeated here. Suffice it to say that the impetus to achieve a manner so personal that it would inevitably set him apart from his contemporaries seems partly to have derived from his acquaintance with French theory. For example, in his *Plans, Elevations and Sections of Buildings*, etc., (1788), he wrote: 'The ingenuity of mankind has hitherto produced only three distinct orders of

8 J. Soane: Bank of England, Waiting Room Courtyard, 1804–05.

9 G. Dance: Project for No. 6 St James's Square, London, c. 1815.

architecture, and perhaps never will invent more, unless such attempts as are shown in "A Proposition for a New Order of Architecture" [published by Henry Emlyn in 1781, reprinted 1784 and 1797] can be considered as increasing the number; yet the Gothic architecture being entirely distinct in all its parts from the Grecian orders gives us some reason to hope. By Gothic architecture I do not mean those barbarous jumbles of undefined forms in modern imitations of Gothic architecture: but the light and elegant examples in many of our cathedrals, churches, and other public buildings.'[14]

It is difficult not to see in this a response to the challenge thrown down by Laugier in Part VI of his *Observations sur l'architecture* (1765), 'De la possibilité d'un nouvel ordre d'Architecture', where he had written arrestingly: 'Prenons le flambeau du génie à la main, pénétrons où les Grecs n'ont point pénétré, et rapportons-en des merveilles inconnues. Il s'agit de créer un nouvel ordre d'Architecture.'[15] The encouragement which Soane derived from what he chose to see as the lightness and grace of Gothic structure, especially as opposed to the trivialities of Picturesque Gothick, may also have been derived directly from French Neoclassical theory. Soane's equivocal reference to the British order of Emlyn's Beaumont Lodge (fig. 7) of c.1790 reminds one that by contrast Soane held up for admiration in his Royal Academy lectures the similarly novel Ammonite order with which Dance adorned the facade of his Shakespeare Gallery in Pall Mall in 1789. The Ammonite order was derived from a suggestion by Piranesi that the original designers of the Ionic order had derived their inspiration from periwinkles.

Despite Dance's interest in Laugier as expressed in his elided entablature at All Hallows Church, despite his interiors like the Guildhall Common Council Chamber and Cranbury Park ballroom with its 'starfish' or cross-vault ceiling, and despite his experimental exteriors at the Guildhall and the Shakespeare Gallery, he never achieved a personal style as coherent and original as Soane's. Nevertheless, their minds interlocked. One of Soane's most original compositions, the north range of the Waiting Room Courtyard at the Bank of England of 1804–05 (fig. 8), is closely paralleled by Dance's unexecuted scheme of c.1815 for No. 6 St James's Square (fig. 9). Soane's building, where for once he achieved a characteristically personal statement in an exterior rather than an interior, is the sophisticated outcome of his search for a primitive and natural architecture inspired by the reactions of Laugier and Chambers to the Vitruvian primitive hut.

The influence of Laugier recurs in the lectures which Soane delivered at the Royal Academy from 1809. Sentiments he had expressed as early as 1788 are echoed in the following pleas: 'Let us remember that everything in Architecture is to be accounted for', and 'nothing can be allowed in good Architecture, for the introduction of which a good reason cannot be assigned.'[16] The following statement shows how close he came to a fundamental attack on the orders: 'I wish to stamp on the mind of the student in Architecture an invariable rule never to be deviated from: namely that wherever columns or parts of columns or any decoration whatever is introduced and can be removed without injuring the strength of the work—such is not true Architecture.'[17] Following Laugier, he condemns unfunctional

10 J. Soane: Bank of England, Princes Street vestibule, 1802.

11 J. Soane: House of Lords, view of one of the Great Rooms, 1822–27.

pediments, even on Perrault's east front of the Louvre and Vardy's Spencer House. Columns and pilasters were not to be combined on the same facade: hence his condemnation of Jones' Banqueting House and Kent's Treasury Buildings. In the interests of naturalness and honesty, the word 'rustication' is taken at face value so that a range of masterpieces including Jones' Banqueting House, Palladio's Palazzo Thiene, Vanbrugh's Scaton Delaval and Grimsthorpe Castle, even Dancc's Newgate Gaol, are condemned for employing it in non-rustic situations.

To conform with Laugier's anti-ornamental principles, Soane was even prepared to censure one of his own finest interiors, the Princes Street vestibule at the Bank of England of 1802 (fig. 10). Illustrating it in his lectures, Soane claimed: 'Had I not been led by the Composition of these Lectures to search into Original Causes and First Principles, the defects in this Design would not have been noticed.' These defects included not only the conjunction of arches with columns, the supposed impropriety of which had been a view dear to Alberti and to French Neoclassical theorists, but also that the elements of the Greek orders 'are here introduced into an interior, which according to the Constructive System of the Greeks belong exclusively to the exterior. It is impossible for me to impress too much on your minds that Modiglions, Mutules, Dentils, and Triglyphs cannot be admitted in the interior of any Edifice with even a shadow of Propriety.'[18] Thus Soane condemns his own noble interiors at Bentley Priory, Tyringham Hall, the proposed House of Lords (fig. 11) and elsewhere.

This same passion for establishing eternal laws of truth,

First Principles, which shall govern all the details of architecture, leads Soane to condemn the use in post-antique classical architecture of all symbolic ornament such as winged figures and lion masks, the caducifer of Mercury, the wings, globes and serpents of pagan worship, the crowns and wreaths of victors in the Olympic Games, gryphons, sphinxes, ox heads, and even egg and dart. All this visual heritage of European classicism—which, ironically, Soane himself deployed so emphatically on the facade of Pitzhanger Manor and in the Old Dividend Office at the Bank of England—is to be consigned to the trash-can because, since the fall of paganism, it has not precisely fulfilled its original functional role: 'such Decorations . . . are only applicable to the mythology and particular customs of the Ancients. It follows, therefore, that they cannot be admitted into the Decoration of Modern Buildings without violating every principle of sound Judgment and correct Taste.'[19] Here again, Soane was echoing views he had held as early as 1788 when he had written: 'The ancients with great propriety decorated their temples and altars with the sculls of victims, rams heads and other ornaments peculiar to their religious ceremonies; but when the same ornaments are introduced in the decoration of English houses, they become puerile and disgusting.'[20]

In adopting so extremist a line, Soane deliberately separated himself from the doctrines of the conservative Sir William Chambers, whose *Treatise on Civil Architecture* of 1759 appeared in new editions in 1768, 1791, 1825 and 1826. In contrast to the theories though scarcely to the practice of Soane, Chambers saw the orders as primarily decorative. Indeed, he discussed them in a book whose title was

12 Percier and Fontaine: Percier staircase at the Louvre, n.d.

13 J. Soane: House of Lords, Scala Regia, c. 1822–27.

expanded in 1791 into *A Treatise on the Decorative Part of Civil Architecture*, and never fulfilled his intention of writing a companion volume on the constructive part containing 'whatever is related to the convenience, strength, or economical management of buildings'.[21] Chambers made a valiant attempt to demolish the mechanical analogy, and therefore justified classical architecture together with its associated ornaments in terms of beauty and association, not of utility and construction: 'Beauty and fitness', he claimed, 'are qualities that have very little connection with each other: in architecture they are sometimes incompatible.'[22] Alive to the decorative charm of pediments, for example, Chambers allowed the presence of more than one of them used as ornamental features where, as in interiors, they carried no suggestion of function. He believed that those who would ban them altogether from interiors 'carry their reasoning too far', adding, as though to clinch the argument, that 'a step further would lead them into the same road with Father Laugier'.[23]

Even in his *Description of the House and Museum on the North Side of Lincoln's Inn Fields* (1835–36), Soane continued to quote from Laugier's *Observations sur l'architecture*.[24] Curiously, the passage he chose concerned the importance of clear and logical planning which Soane regretted he had been unable to achieve fully at Lincoln's Inn Fields because of his gradual acquisition of the site. In 1819 Soane had made an extended visit to Paris where he especially admired the noble scale of the Tuileries and the Louvre. The interiors by Percier and Fontaine that he would have seen in these palaces seem to have influenced

the flashy classicism of his Scala Regia and Royal Gallery at the House of Lords in 1822–24 (figs. 12,13). In Percier and Fontaine's *Recueil de décorations intérieures* (1812) he would also have found two plates showing the impact of mirrors incorporated architecturally into domestic interiors in Spain and Poland, a device he deployed so brilliantly in the Soane Museum. When in Rome as a young man he had visited the Villa Albani, the celebrated house-cum-museum designed by Carlo Marchionni in c.1760, where he made particular note[25] of the setting of statues in niches lined with mirrors, the incorporation of antique bas-reliefs into the architectural setting, and the corbels ornamented with rams' skulls and imitation metopes. It is less easy to relate Soane to the architecture than to the theory of Neoclassical France for the simple reason that he seems to have had virtually no French contemporaries. In other words, no French architect of major importance was born in the 1750s. Ledoux, de Wailly, Peyre, Antoine, Chalgrin, Louis, Gondoin and Brongniart were all born in the 1730s. The 1760s saw the birth of architects like Durand, Percier and Fontaine who all seem to belong to a later world than Soane. An exception is provided by the boldly independent architect Thomas de Thomon, born in 1754, but his removal to St Petersburg in 1790 makes further comparison inappropriate.

The difficulty of relating so individual an architect as Soane to the architecture of his time is heightened by the fact that his most productive period in 1793–1815 coincided with the Napoleonic Wars: in other words, a time when architectural practice in the country as a whole was cut to a minimum.

14 T. Leverton: No. 1 Bedford Square, London, c. 1775.

15 J. Tasker: St Mary, East Lulworth, Dorset, 1786–87.

Soane was exceptional in finding in the Bank of England an employer with building requirements which increased as the war continued and the national debt accumulated. He was also fortunate in meeting wealthy patrons through the Bank and in being able to indulge himself in these years in elaborately remodelling his private residence in Lincoln's Inn Fields. By the time that the building profession was able to expand rapidly from 1815, Soane had adopted an even more eccentric version of his personal style, for example in the Law Courts, which naturally found no imitators. Apart from the work of Dance, the earliest interiors suggesting that other architects were moving along similar lines to Soane are the entrance hall at No. 1 Bedford Square of c.1775 (fig. 14), attributed to Thomas Leverton, and the Catholic church at Lulworth, Dorset of 1786–87 by John Tasker (fig. 15). These floating flowing spaces derive from the Picturesque revolution in planning which Robert Adam had effected when he deliberately dissolved the four-square solidity of Palladian apartments. The central division in Leverton's tripartite hall has an oval dome with umbrella ribs on plain pendentives and is flanked on one side by an oval staircase and on the other by an apsed vestibule. The flow of space through these three areas is interrupted as little as possible by features such as cornices which are almost completely elided. Just as Soane at the Bank designed domed spaces which had no exterior architecture, so Tasker at Lulworth had to design a substantial church with as little external display as possible. What looks at first like a Tuscan garden temple turns out to be a sizeable church on a quatrefoil plan with a central domed space flanked by three segmental apses and one semi-circular one. There is an unexpected connection between Lulworth church and the Catholic Cathedral at Baltimore, Maryland (fig. 16) of 1805–18 by Benjamin Latrobe (1764–1820), who, after Dance, is perhaps the architect closest stylistically to Soane. The connection is that John Carroll, first Bishop of Baltimore, was consecrated in Lulworth church in 1790. Like Lulworth, Latrobe's lovely interior is centrally planned with a domed space supported on segmental arches and with galleries in the arms of the cross. Latrobe had worked from 1784 to 1790 in the office of Soane's exact contemporary S. P. Cockerell (1753–1827), one of the most original architects of the day. In the remarkable tower which he added to St Anne's, Soho (fig. 17), in 1802 Cockerell handled planes of brick and stone, segmental openings and curious sculptural forms in a manner directly analagous to Soane. Latrobe left England for America in 1796, but when one considers the top-lit domed rotunda at his now demolished Greek Revival Bank of Pennsylvania in Philadelphia (1798–1800), it is hard not to imagine that he had seen Soane's early interiors in the Bank of England. Similar domed spaces occur in his (unexecuted) Library at Baltimore of 1818 and his Exchange in the same city designed in the following year.

Latrobe came closest to Soane in the interiors he provided at the Capitol Building in Washington, begun in 1792 by William Thornton and others. Interested in the creation of a new order of architecture, like Laugier, Emlyn, Dance and Soane, Latrobe formed a Soane-like vestibule in the east basement in 1809 (rebuilt by him after the fire of 1814), which contained capitals of a novel American maize-leaf

16 B. Latrobe: Catholic Cathedral, Baltimore, Maryland, 1805–18.

17 S. P. Cockerell: St Anne's, Soho, London, 1802.

18 B. Latrobe: Capitol Building, Washington D.C., vestibule with maize-leaf capitals, 1809.

19 B. Latrobe: Supreme Court Chamber, Washington D.C., 1815–17.

type (fig. 18). Elsewhere, he provided a small rotunda with tobacco-leaf capitals, but his most striking interior was the Supreme Court Chamber (fig. 19) of 1815–17, based on plans made as early as 1806–07. A curiously lobed semi-dome rests on a trio of coffered arches supported by primitivist Doric columns. This unprecedented architecture is comparable only to certain works by Ledoux and Soane, though Wyatt had more than hinted at it in the ribbed octagonal hall of his Radcliffe Observatory at Oxford of 1776 onwards:

Soane's famous contemporary John Nash (1752–1835) is superficially close to him as an exponent of the Picturesque, but tremendously far from him in all fundamentals. Both men incorporated the doctrines of Price and Knight yet in such different ways that it is not merely a truism but a serious response to their aesthetic intentions to repeat the view that one thinks of Nash in terms of exteriors and Soane of interiors. An exception is afforded by the top-lit galleries which Nash provided at his own house, Nos 14–16 Regent Street (1822–24), and at Buckingham Palace (1825–30), a commission which by rights should have gone to Soane (figs. 20,21). The gallery at Buckingham Palace contained aisles which were defined by strange pendant arches obviously inspired by those Soane had provided in his dining room at Lincoln's Inn Fields and in the Court of Chancery at Westminster. Alas, the glazed domes in Nash's side compartments shed light on the floor not on the pictures, so that the room was completely remodelled by Aston Webb in 1914.

Perhaps in attempting to relate Soane to the architecture of his time we are following a false trail, and that with so complete a poet-architect we should be looking rather at Wordsworth, Beethoven and Turner. It could surely be maintained that no architect was as close in artistic vision to Soane as the painter J. M. W. Turner (1778–1851).[26] The preoccupation with light is central to both, as it had also been to Dance. Soane's dissolution of conventional architectural forms into a series of poetically-lit hollowed-out spaces is surely a parallel to Turner's late style. Turner's deep feeling for architecture and his friendship with architects such as Dance, Soane and C. R. Cockerell is a subject which should be explored. He had been trained in perspective by the draughtsman Thomas Malton and in architecture by Soane's old friend Thomas Hardwick. The plates in Soane's *Sketches in Architecture* (1793), especially the foliage and vegetation, and the watercolours produced in his office at this time, are close to the work of Malton and Turner. The pictorial representation of architecture by means of fetching watercolours, in which Turner was a pioneer, was a natural product of Picturesque sensibility which had been further stimulated by a desire to save the expense of models on the part of those exhibiting architectural projects at the Royal Academy. Soane complained to the Royal Academy in 1807 that no lectures on perspective had been delivered for many years. In February 1807 his assistant Gandy offered to deliver the lectures but in December that year Turner was appointed Professor of Perspective. He was not ready to deliver his first lecture until January 1811, having prepared nearly two hundred large drawings and diagrams to demonstrate his preoccu-

20 J. Nash: Buckingham Palace, picture gallery, 1825–30.

21 J. Nash: Own house, Nos 14–16 Regent Street, London, 1822–24.

22 J. M. W. Turner: 'Solus Lodge', Twickenham, 1810–12 (engraving by W. B. Cooke, 1814, after a drawing by W. Havell).

pation with coloured light and reflections. Ruskin wrote admiringly of these that 'elaborate attention is always paid to the disposition of shadows and (especially) reflected lights. Huge perspectives and elevations of the Dome of St. Paul's lie in this portfolio side by side with studies of the reflections on glass balls; and measured gleams of moonlight on the pillar of Trajan, with dispositions of chiaroscuro cast by the gaoler's lantern on the passages of Newgate.'[27] Ruskin's words were prompted by Turner's coloured studies of reflection and refraction based, for example, on the juxtaposition of glass balls, some empty and some half-filled with water. Is it too romantic for us to find a parallel here to Soane's late interiors with their diaphanous lighting effects, mirrors and coloured glass?

In 1806, Soane had become Professor of Architecture at the Royal Academy and in 1809 we find Turner helping him by organizing the showing of the drawings prepared by Soane to illustrate his lectures which began that March. In 1811 Turner modified the lighting in the lecture room for the benefit of both his and Soane's lecture illustrations. Turner's preoccupation with light in painting was thus appropriately accompanied by a concern for the proper display of pictures which he also shared with Soane. In 1803 Turner visited the new top-lit Truchsessian Gallery in London[28] and opened his own private gallery at No. 64 Harley Street in the following year. He presumably knew Soane's important top-lit picture gallery of 1787 at Fonthill House and in 1804 returned two drawings to Soane which it is tempting to suggest may have been related to lighting arrangements. With these drawings, Turner sent as a gift an aquatint after a watercolour by himself of the interior of Wyatt's mausoleum at Brocklesby Park, Lincolnshire (1787–94), a windowless rotunda top-lit through a dome of painted glass. He subsequently referred to the refraction of light through

this lantern in his Royal Academy lecture on 'Light, Shade and Reflexes', first delivered in 1815.

In 1810–12 Turner built a little Italianate house[29] for himself at Sandycombe Lodge, Twickenham (fig. 22)—the kind of picturesquely sited chalet which Ruskin was later to admire in his 'The Poetry of Architecture; or the Architecture of the Nations of Europe considered in its Association with natural Scenery and national Character', published in Loudon's *Architectural Magazine* in 1837–38. At the same time, the building has a certain Soanean flavour both inside and out, especially in the detailing of the entrance hall with its tall thin arches. At No. 46 Queen Anne Street West, Turner built himself a second picture gallery in 1819–21 which he seems to have discussed with Soane from as early as 1815. Opened in 1822, it was a long narrow room, top-lit with octagonal skylights and walls covered with the dull red drapery then popular for galleries. The skylights were inspired by Soane's at Dulwich, though on his visit to the Louvre in 1819 Turner had also made careful drawings of the Grande Galerie following its recent remodelling with top lights. In 1832 Turner even considered turning his own house into a permanent Turner Museum along similar lines to those which Soane was adopting at that moment, which Thomas Hope had achieved at Duchess Street by 1804 and which Sir Francis Bourgeois had proposed nearby in Charlotte (now Hallam) Street in 1810.

In Soane's eighth lecture at the Royal Academy, first delivered in 1815, he remarked that: 'In Galleries . . . light is often introduced very advantageously above the Cornice, so that the window is not seen from below: by this contrivance a pleasing kind of demi-tint is thrown over the whole surface of the Ceiling',[30] a point he illustrated with a section of Dance's gallery at Lansdowne House. Apart

23 J. Leicester: Own house, No. 24 Hill Street, London, c. 1806, gallery.

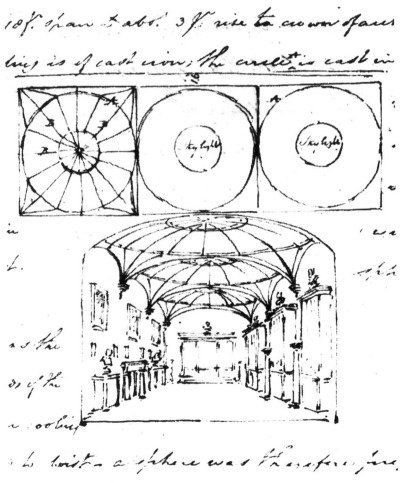

24 R. Payne Knight: Own house, No. 3 Soho Square, London, 1809, plan
and perspective sketches of gallery-cum-library.

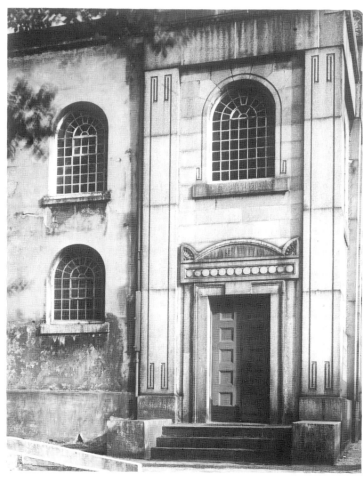

25 J. Foulston: St Andrew's Chapel, Plymouth, Devon, 1823, exterior.

26 J. Foulston: St Andrew's Chapel, Plymouth, Devon, 1823, interior.

from Turner's second gallery there were at least two more in London which were closely related to Soane's work. In c.1806 Sir John Leicester, Bt., patron, collector and early admirer of Turner, created a strikingly Soanean gallery at his London house at No. 24 Hill Street (fig. 23).[31] The design of this room, which was open to the public, has been attributed to Thomas Cundy (1765–1825), although its closeness to Soane's gallery at Fonthill House suggests that Soane may have been involved. We should also note the remarkable gallery-cum-library at No. 3 Soho Square (fig. 24) built in 1809 for Richard Payne Knight, presumably to his own specifications, by a builder named Andrews. With its ceiling vaulted in three domed bays entirely of cast-iron and glass, Payne Knight's gallery was especially admired by C. R. Cockerell whose drawing of it is, incidentally, the only known record of its existence.[32] It is interesting to find a top-lit interior differing strikingly from Soane in its lack of clerestory lighting, yet designed by the Picturesque theorist whose *Analytical Enquiry into the Principles of Taste* (1805) Soane had studied and annotated. A closer parallel to Soane is afforded by the work of John Foulston (1772–1842) who carried his style to the west country, most notably in three now demolished buildings: the Proprietary Library (1812) and St Andrew's Chapel (1823, figs. 25,26) at Plymouth, and the Public Ballroom (1830) at Torquay. James Spiller (c.1760–1829), a pupil of James Wyatt, was closely associated with Soane, 'who occasionally employed him to survey or supervise works in his care'. His most striking independent work was St John's

Church, Hackney of 1792–97, with porches and a bizarre Soanean Baroque steeple added from his own designs in 1812–13. Its Greek cross plan allows for transepts on three sides with galleries supported by Greek Doric columns and, floating over the central space, a shallow vault resting on segmental arches. Soane's pupil David Laing (1774–1856) published *Hints for Dwellings* (1804) with numerous fanciful details of an ultimately Soanean derivation, and built the much more serious Custom House in Thames Street, London, in 1813–17 (figs. 27,28). This elegant and original building contained the triple-domed Long Room with a flavour at once Parisian and Soanean. Unfortunately this attractive interior was completely altered by Smirke when he rebuilt the whole building in 1825–27 after the embarrassing collapse of its central portion.

It might be supposed that Soane would have welcomed what Pugin condemned as 'the New Square Style of Mr. Smirke' as a parallel to the linearity of his own style. That he did not is testified by his celebrated attack on Smirke's Covent Garden Theatre in a Royal Academy lecture of 1810. Soane had specially prepared two large drawings of the theatre so as to emphasize one of the defects of much Greek Revival architecture: the lack of relationship between the principal façade, dominated by a monumental portico, and the more economically designed side and rear elevations.

It is tempting to assume that Soane would have been more

27 D. Laing: The Long Room of the Custom House, Thames Street, London, 1813–17.

28 D. Laing: Design for a villa from *Hints for Dwellings*, 1804.

29 J. Wyatville: Bretton Hall, Yorkshire, c. 1815, vestibule looking towards the staircase hall.

30 J. Dobson: Longhirst, Northumberland, 1824–28.

31 W. J. Donthorn: Elmham Hall, Norfolk, 1830.

32 J. Soane: Tyringham Hall, Buckinghamshire, entrance lodge, 1794.

33 F. Gilly: Project for a Monument to Frederick the Great, 1797.

34. G. Dance: Coleorton Hall, Leicestershire, 1804, south elevation.

35 K. F. Schinkel: Project for a bazaar in Unter den Linden, Berlin, 1827.

sympathetic to the work of Thomas Harrison (1744–1829) and John Dobson (1787–1865) who sustained Neoclassical ideals in the north and north-west of England. With Harrison it is not the presence of romantic top-lit interiors which recalls Soane, but rather his total dedication to architecture and the absolute conviction which is stamped on every stone of his buildings. His early career was similar to Soane's: he came from a humble background but his skill as a draughtsman enabled him to find a patron willing to support him in Rome where he stayed from 1769–76, entering for the annual architectural prize offered by the Accademia de San Luca in 1773. Like Soane, he never forgot the grand manner of international Neoclassicism and produced visionary designs for a national Walhalla in c.1814–15. An isolated example of a Soanean interior occurs at Bretton Hall, Yorkshire, where Wyatville provided a spectacular hall and staircase in c.1815 (fig. 29), adorned with vast ruin-paintings by Agostino Aglio so as to form a romantic composition which is powerfully evocative of Gandy's Picturesque paintings of Soane's work. The shallow-domed halls and staircases of John Dobson's classical mansions in Northumberland, such as Longhirst and Nunneykirk of the 1820s (fig. 30), are variants of themes close to Soane's heart. The abstract reductionist element in Soane's style was taken to extremes by a pupil of Wyatville's, the Norfolk architect W. J. Donthorn (1799–1859).[33] The most striking examples of his elementalist approach are his designs of c.1830 for three Norfolk houses—Westacre High House, Watlington Hall and Elmham Hall (fig. 31). The trabeated austerity of the wings he added to Elmham recalls warehouse design in that, following Laugier, the wall has been replaced by glazed areas separated by piers. Now this is immediately reminiscent of Schinkel and indeed there are close affinities between Soane and the Franco-Prussian style of around 1800: the style, that is, of architects like the elder and the younger Gilly, Gentz and the youthful Weinbrenner who were profoundly affected by Ledoux, especially his *barrières*. The bare geometrical forms of Soane's lodge at Tyringham Hall (1794) are echoed in the gateway to Friedrich Gilly's Monument to Frederick the Great (1797) or in Weinbrenner's sketches made in Rome in the 1790s (figs. 32,33). George Dance, as might be expected, is also close to this tradition. His drawing of 1804 for the south front of Coleorton Hall,

Leicestershire, is a grid-like composition in which the wall has been entirely dissolved (fig. 34). As a daring example of what Dance proposed as 'Architecture unshackled', it can be compared with Schinkel's project of 1827 for a bazaar in Unter den Linden, Berlin (fig. 35).

Born in 1781, Schinkel was a generation younger than Soane and because of the Napoleonic Wars his career as an architect did not begin until after 1815. He is akin to Soane in the total dedication of his entire life, professional and social, to what mattered to him most, architecture; and also in the handling of architectural forms so as to produce effects which are now linear and astringent, now Picturesque and poetical. The hints which Soane gave in buildings like Butterton Farm House, Staffordshire (1815–16) were developed by Schinkel in, for example, his Military Prison in the Lindenstrasse, Berlin (1817) so as to create a rationalist brick architecture with the orders reduced to an apparently constructional grid (figs. 36–39). However, as an architect who believed like Soane in the 'Poetry of Architecture', Schinkel was intrigued by the Soane Museum on his visit in June 1826. He recorded in his journal[34] the Picturesque planning, the small passages and the romantic effects produced by top and side lighting. Hittorff was later to share this appreciation in a paper on the Soane Museum which he delivered at the Société Libre des Beaux-Arts in Paris in November 1836. At the Bank of England, Schinkel found 'much useless stuff', though he greatly admired the triumphal archway, modelled on the Arch of Constantine, on the south side of the Lothbury Court. In this preference he is identical to C. R. Cockerell who similarly admired the archway while finding 'the lantern rooms all subject to inconvenience of air descending on the head . . . Corridores are narrow & petites but highly studied & some beautiful effect.' However, he felt that the overall impression was at once 'little & great, the taste sometimes flat, sometimes unreasonably bold'.[35] When in 1834 Cockerell was called on to provide a new Dividend Pay Office at the Bank he produced an impressive colonnaded interior with high top lighting which represents a successful attempt at working in Soane's manner while eliminating his meretricious detail. These elements in Soane's work had always attracted criticism. In August 1796 Farington recorded that 'Soane's architecture at the

36 K. F. Schinkel: Schauspielhaus, Berlin, 1819–21, the north facade.

37 J. Soane: Bank of England, detail of the Threadneedle Street facade.

Bank was described to be affected and contemptible', while another contemporary critic found it 'ribbed like loins of pork'. In 1824 there was a more sustained and serious attack on his work in an article entitled 'The Sixth or Boetian Order of Architecture' in *Knight's Quarterly Magazine*. Cockerell, too, was especially harsh on Soane's Law Courts at Westminster, writing of them in his diary in 1826: 'thought them trivial, absurd in their architecture, should not expect to hear Sense in such foolish Rooms'.[36]

In *The Public Buildings of London* (2 vols, 1825–28), W. H. Leeds and Soane's old admirer John Britton took a far more sympathetic line in their accounts of Soane's Bank of England, Law Courts, House of Lords entrance, Privy Council and Board of Trade Offices, and Soane Museum. In his somewhat over-effusive description of the Bank, Leeds repeatedly praised its 'picturesque' effects, its 'architectural scenery' and its perfect expression of 'the *poetry* of the art' of architecture.[37]

However, by the time of his death in 1837 Soane's reputation had rapidly declined. On his tour of England in 1832 the German critic J. D. Passavant condemned the meretricious Picturesque effects of both Nash and Soane and even of C. R. Cockerell's Hanover Chapel. He complained of the Bank of England that: 'As far as regards individual parts, it is strictly Grecian, but the little injudicious additions and interruptions of style he has fallen into, produce a confused effect, reminding us of the buildings by Van Brugh.'[38] His preference was for Schinkel and consequently for Smirke, whose General Post Office he was surprisingly prepared to compare in quality with Schinkel's Altes Museum; he was also open to the more adaptable *Rundbogenstil* proposed by Hübsch in his essay of 1828, *In welchem Styl sollen wir bauen?* In his *Review of the*

Professional Life of Sir John Soane (1837), T. L. Donaldson sharply censured Soane's late works with the exception of his State Paper Office of 1829–33, an Italianate palazzo on the edge of St James's Park. However, even here an Early Victorian fondness for rich texture led Donaldson to write that the 'details of his facades only require greater vigor and boldness of profile in order to make this edifice rank with the masterpieces of Italian art'.[39] Pugin attacked the Soane Museum in the first edition of *Contrasts* in 1836 and the nadir was reached, as is often the case with the reputation of architects, in the years immediately following his death. Thus in each of the first four volumes from 1837–41 of the newly-founded *Civil Engineer and Architect's Journal*, an organ with a no-nonsense professional air, the Soane Museum and the Act of Parliament by which it was vested in the nation were dismissed as tomfoolery. The author made the interesting criticism that the building contained 'much also that looks no better than a temporary experimental trial or model of what was intended to be executed on a larger scale: for at present, not a few effects partake of far too much of the petty and the peep-show'.[40] In 1839, the anonymous critic drew attention to the irony by which the typical modern facade, constructed of little more than lath and plaster, generally managed to look substantial, whereas for the facade of the Soane Museum 'stone has been employed to form a flimsy-looking fabric, whose frame is scarcely thicker than a wall of stout planks'.[41] Neither the practical Schinkel nor the generous Cockerell ever adopted the narrow passages and the small openings which in Soane's later work seem to be related to his escape from hostility and disappointment. It may be appropriate to leave Soane in Lincoln's Inn Fields, nursing resentments within his marble mouse-trap, since we thereby emphasize his isolation from contemporaries with whom, as we have seen, he had so little in common.

38 K. F. Schinkel: Military Prison and Barracks, Lindenstrasse, Berlin, 1817.

NOTES

In the preparation of this paper I am much indebted to discussions with Sir John Summerson, Mr John Harris, Dr John Gage and Mr G.-Tilman Mellinghoff.

1 Although, as Sir John Summerson points out to me, when one juxtaposes Soane's schemes with actual Grand Prix projects they separate 'like oil and water'.

2 Letter dated 13 June 1807, published in Hoare's *The Artist*, i, 1810, No. xiv, p. 8.

3 P. de la Ruffinière du Prey, 'Soane and Hardwick in Rome: a Neoclassical partnership', *Architectural History*, xv, 1972, pp. 51–67.

4 D. Stroud, 'Soane's Design for a Triumphal Bridge', *Architectural Review*, April 1957, pp. 260–62.

5 D. Stillman, 'British Architects and Italian Architectural Competitions, 1758–1780', *Journal of the Society of Architectural Historians* (U.S.A.), xxxii, 1973, pp. 43–66.

6 J. Harris, 'Robert Mylne and the Academy of St. Luke', *Architectural Review*, November 1961, pp. 341–42.

7 J. Soane, *Designs for Public and Private Buildings*, 1828, p. 25.

8 *Boullée's Treatise on Architecture*, ed. H. Rosenau, 1953, p. 51. 'It is light that produces impressions... If I could avoid direct light and arrange for its presence without the onlooker being aware of its source, the ensuing effects of mysterious daylight would produce inconceivable impressions...'

9 P. de la Ruffinière du Prey, 'John Soane's Architectural Education, 1753–80' (Princeton Ph.D. dissertation 1972), 1977.

10 J. Soane, *Description of the House and Museum*, etc., 1835–36, p. 54.

11 *Boullée's Treatise, op. cit.*, p. 26. 'Our buildings, above all our public buildings, ought in some way to be poems.'

12 I. Ware, *Complete Body of Architecture*, 1756, p. 136.

13 J. Soane, *Plans, Elevations and Sections of Buildings*, etc., 1788, p. 8.

14 *Ibid.*, p. 9.

15 M. A. Laugier, *Observations sur l'architecture*, 1765, p. 253. 'Let us take the torch of genius in our hands, penetrate those areas untouched by the Greeks, and draw out unknown marvels. It is a matter of creating a new order of architecture.'

16 J. Soane, *Lectures on Architecture*, ed. A. T. Bolton, 1929, pp. 45 and 85.

17 Soane's lecture notes, quoted from W. Herrmann,

39 J. Soane: Butterton Farm House, Staffordshire, 1815–16, watercolour. (FO. v. 94)

Laugier and 18th century French Theory, 1962, p. 182.

18 J. Soane, *Lectures*, *op. cit.*, p. 95. Summerson suggests to me that having flayed Smirke in his RA lectures in 1810, Soane now flayed himself simply to show how fair-minded he could be.

19 *Ibid.*, p. 100.

20 J. Soane, *Plans, Elevations and Sections of Buildings*, etc., p. 9.

21 W. Chambers, *Treatise* (1791 edition), p. 135.

22 *Ibid.*, p. 99.

23 *Ibid.*, pp. 98–99.

24 On p. 2 Soane quotes from Laugier's *Observations*, *op. cit.*, p. 152.

25 P. de la Ruffinière du Prey, Ph.D. dissertation, p. 272.

26 In the following paragraphs I have drawn heavily on J. Gage, *Colour in Turner*, 1969.

27 *The Works of John Ruskin*, Library Edition, xiii, 1904, p. 308.

28 See *Monthly Magazine*, xvi, 1803, pp. 257–59 and 470.

29 A. Livermore, 'Sandycombe Lodge, "Turner's little house at Twickenham"', *Country Life*, 6 July 1951, pp. 40–42.

30 J. Soane, *Lectures*, *op. cit.*, p. 126.

31 See *Magazine of the Fine Arts*, i, 1821, pp. 54–57.

32 J. Harris, 'C.R. Cockerell's "Ichnographica Domestica"', *Architectural History*, xiv, 1971, p. 20 and fig. 15(b).

33 R. McD. O'Donnell, 'W.J. Donthorn (1799–1859): architecture with "great hardness and decision at the edges"', *Architectural History*, xxi, 1978, pp. 83–96.

34 A. von Wolzogen, *Aus Schinkel's Nachlass*, 4 vols, Berlin 1862–64, ii, pp. 137–65.

35 D.J. Watkin, *The Life and Work of C.R. Cockerell, R.A.*, 1974, p. 67.

36 *Ibid.*

37 J. Britton, A.C. Pugin *et al.*, *The Public Buildings of London*, 2 vols, 1825–28, ii, pp. 245 and 253.

38 J.D. Passavant, *Tour of a German Artist in England*, 2 vols, 1836, ii, p. 303.

39 T.L. Donaldson, *Review of the Professional Life of Sir John Soane*, 1837, p. 22.

40 *Civil Engineer and Architect's Journal*, i, 1837–38, p. 44.

41 *Ibid.*, ii, 1839, p. 304.

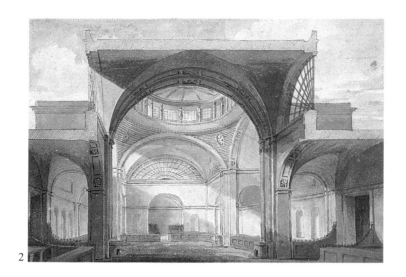

The Bank of England

John Soane was appointed Architect to the Bank of England in October 1788 with the support of the then Prime Minister William Pitt, from a group of fifteen competitors who included James Wyatt, Henry Holland, S. P. Cockerell and Charles Beazley. The position, which was to be the longest-held and most important of his lifetime, placed Soane's career on a firm financial footing and gave him important professional status. In this office, he succeeded Sir Robert Taylor (1765–88), who had in turn replaced George Sampson, the creator of the original Bank building 'in a grand style of Palladian simplicity' (1732).[1]

The plan of the Bank developed over a period of time as adjacent properties were acquired and extensions and replacements built. Soane, knitting the old to the new with great ingenuity, left, at his retirement in 1833, a highly complex building contained within a continuous wall, designed by himself.

The rebuilding fell into three broadly distinct periods, beginning with the Bank Stock Office in 1792 and the external screen walls at the end of Bartholomew Lane, the main front then facing Lothbury and only half its present length. The rebuilding of the Bank Stock Office, made necessary by the discovery of damp-infested roof timbers, is arguably the first manifestation of what has been termed the Soane style.[2] The new office was built entirely of incombustible materials, namely brick arches springing from stone piers and vaulted with hollow earthenware 'cones' to lighten the superstructure. A large domed space with a twelve-sided lantern light was flanked by narrow aisles, each lit by semi-circular windows or lunettes. The orders were dispensed with in favour of pilaster-strips, a fretted string-course substituting for the usual entablature and finished with delicate plaster ornamentation, including the characteristic Soanean *paterae* and scoring of the spandrils. The effect was one of a free and primitive classicism stripped of its later embellishments. The Bank Stock Office was to become the model for several later essays within the Bank, notably the Four and Five Per Cent Office (1794), Consols Office (1797) and Colonial and Dividend Offices (1818). The Rotunda (originally the Stock Exchange), fifty-seven feet in diameter and equal in height, was built between 1794 and 1796, and is a striking instance of Soane's gift for lofty interiors. Lothbury Court (1797), also of the same phase, was one of nine internal courts, and as built was the result of numerous preliminary studies by Soane based on Palladio and the Antique.

During the middle period, 1800–18, Princes Street was extended in a straight line to Lothbury. The famous Tivoli Corner was so called because its order (which was that of the earlier screen walls) derived from the Temple of Vesta at Tivoli.[3]

1 Lothbury Court, seen from Residence Court, 1798–99. (Dr. xii. 3. 14)

2 Sectional view of the Consols Office, 1798–99. (Fo. v. 64)

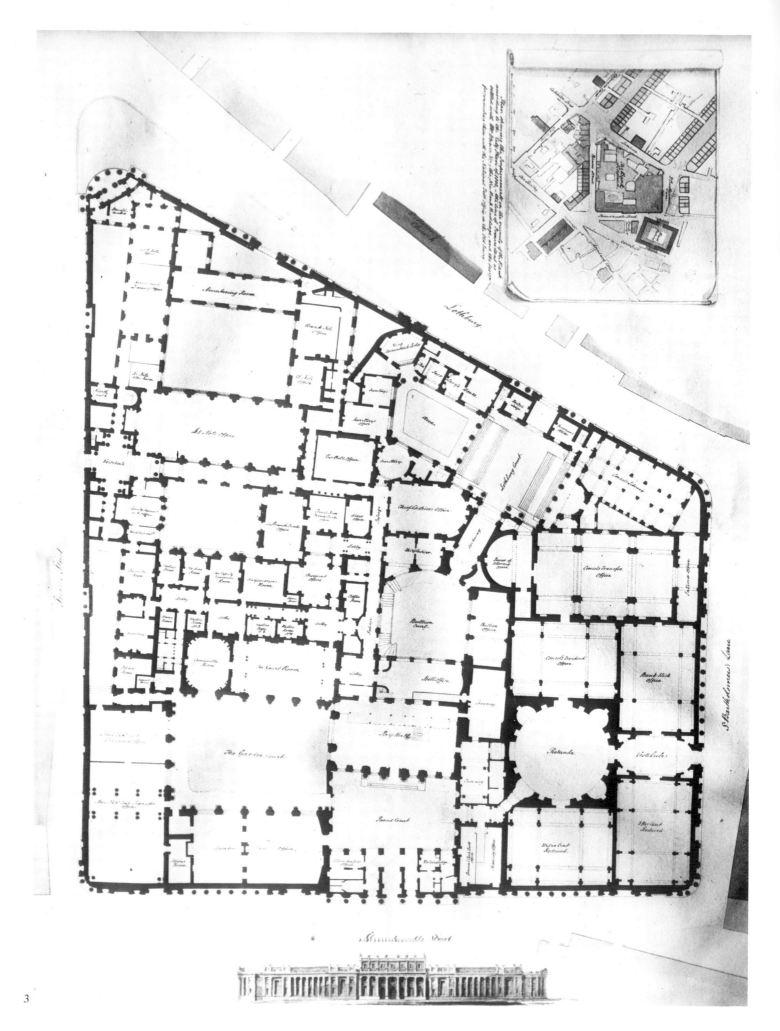

3 Plan of the Bank of England as completed by Soane, with the elevation to Threadneedle Street and an inset site plan. Soane's main halls, 1792–94 and 1818, are grouped round the Rotunda on the right (east). As further property was acquired Soane introduced two new axes—a north-east axis through Lothbury Court, 1797–98, and an east-west axis through the Princes Street entrance on the west, 1804. (Dance cabinet)

4 Soane's preliminary sketches for the south side of Lothbury Court, 1797. These were superseded by an arch modelled on the Arch of Titus in Rome but with an order of Soane's invention, based partly on the Temple of Vesta at Tivoli; a larger and elaborated version of the order which he used for the exterior walls of the Bank. Lothbury Court is one of the few interior parts of Soane's Bank still standing. (Dr. x. 3. 5)

The third and final phase saw the rebuilding of the Threadneedle Street facade, together with the southern part of Princes Street and Bartholomew Lane (1823–26). Threadneedle Street, because of its lower level, is generally thought to be weaker in its impact than the earlier work by Soane at the rear of the building.

Soane eventually resigned from his office at the Bank in 1833 as a result of failing eyesight. The building by now covered a site of three acres, and during the forty-five years of construction and continuous repairs by Soane had cost an estimated £860,000[4]—£30 million at least in today's terms.

The Bank survived with some alterations until 1930, during which decade it was largely rebuilt under Sir Herbert Baker. Today, the screen wall is still largely intact, though the Tivoli Corner has been penetrated by a pedestrian thoroughfare. A few parts of the interior also survive. The exact workings of the Bank as Soane conceived it are difficult to envisage, a whole series of changes having overlaid the original intentions prior to the demolition of the 1930s.

Notes

1 A. Bolton, *The Works of Sir John Soane, R.A.*, London 1924, pp. 32–68.
2 See Sir John Summerson's essay above, especially pages 10–16 for an extended discussion of the Bank Stock Office.
3 D. Stroud, *The Architecture of Sir John Soane*, London 1961, pp. 65–78.
4 Bolton, *op.cit.*, pp. 60–68.

5 Aerial cut-away perspective of the Bank of England as completed by Soane.

Drawing by J. M. Gandy, exhibited at the RA in 1830. (N. Drg. Rm.)

6, 7 Part of the central colonnade of the Threadneedle Street facade, 1825–27, and colonnade, east side of Lothbury Court, 1798–99.

8 Lothbury Court, seen from Residence Court, 1798–99.

9 South side Governor's Court, 1804–05.

10 Colonnade, east side of Lothbury Court, 1798–99.

11 The loggia forming the north side of Governor's Court, 1804–05.

12 Front to Bartholomew Lane and return to Lothbury, 1823–25. (Dr. xii. 1. 4)

13 The Lothbury front as first built, 1795. It was doubled in length 1803–05, see p. 69. (Dr. xii. 1. 1)

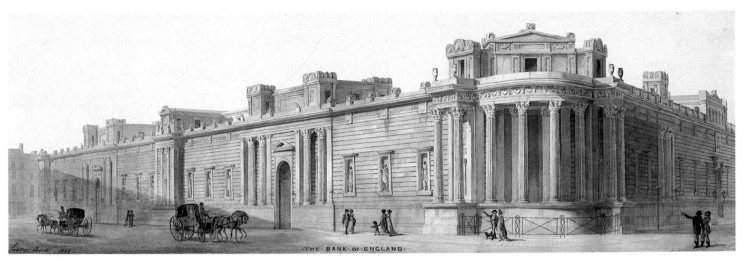

14 View from north-west showing the Lothbury front as completed in 1805. (Dr. xii. 1. 2)

15 Progress drawing of the vault of the Old Colonial or Five Per Cent Office, 1818, showing construction with earthenware 'cones'. (Dr. ii. 3. 4c)

16 The vestibule at the Princes Street entrance, 1804–05.

17 The Bank Stock Office, 1792–93.

18, 19 The Consols Office, 1798–99.

20 Design for the Consols Office, 1798. (Dr. xi. 4. 3)

21 Progress drawings of the Consols Office before plastering. By J. M.Gandy, 1799. (Dr. xi. 6. 2)

22 The Rotunda. Drawing by J. M. Gandy, 1798. (Dr. ix. 2)

23 The Old Dividend Office, 1818–23.

24 The Old £5 Note Office, 1805–06.

25 The Dividend Pay Office designed in 1849 by Soane's successor, C. R. Cockerell.

26 Statue of Sir John Soane on the Lothbury front of the Bank. By Sir Charles Wheeler, c. 1935.

27 The Old £5 Note Office, 1805–06.

THE PICTURE GALLERY

G.-TILMAN MELLINGHOFF

SOANE'S

Dulwich Picture Gallery *Revisited*

DULWICH GALLERY was designed by Soane in 1811 when he had reached the prime of life and had attained his very own inward-looking style. It is regarded by Summerson as 'the apex of his achievement' and indeed Dulwich was a work particularly dear to Soane, to which he devoted great personal energy.[1] The sheer quantity, variety and inconsistency of the surviving plans alone give this impression. Moreover they reflect the quintessence of Soane's innermost belief that architecture is 'an Art purely of Invention, and Invention is the most painful and the most difficult exercise of the human mind'.[2] Despite the signal importance of the Dulwich Gallery in Soane's career it has not been given the attention it deserves.[3] This article can provide only a rather condensed view of the complex history of the building. Its prime purpose is to elucidate Dulwich's complicated design process and to show how Soane felt impelled to create a unique monument for his close friend Sir Peter Francis Bourgeois and his enlightened bequest of 360 pictures to Dulwich College.

In fact, Bourgeois' only instruction had been the erection of a mausoleum at Dulwich 'as far as possible of marble'[4] and copied from that Soane had built for him in 1807 at Charlotte (now Hallam) Street to receive the remains of his

life companion Noel Desenfans, the originator of the collection. As for the pictures, Bourgeois had less ambitious ideas. There he had merely thought of adapting the old College gallery, which had since 1764 been in the upper west wing of the three-sided, early seventeenth-century quadrangle next to the school rooms, almshouses and chapel (fig. 3).[5] The gallery's existence had after all been one of the reasons for Bourgeois' choice of Dulwich. 'For the repairing, improving and beautifying' of this gallery wing he had set aside £2,000 in his will.[6] This was hardly the sum for a new building. However, it seems quite likely that Soane already had dreams of a new building when he went to inspect the College on January 8th, 1811. There were good reasons for this. Because of the appalling state of the College buildings the authorities had only three years previously arranged by Act of Parliament to raise funds primarily for 'repairing the said College, or rebuilding the same, either on the present site or on such other part . . . belonging to the same College'.[7] Rebuilding was indeed in Soane's mind when he presented in May 1811 five different designs for a totally new College quadrangle, in which he retained only the chapel (figs. 4, 9–13). Yet his ambitious and, for the period of the Napoleonic Wars, obviously extravagant scheme was rejected. Perhaps he was already

1 Vista through the newly built galleries, a watercolour by J. M. Gandy. The actual wall colour, however, was 'something like burnt oker' according to the advice of the President of the Royal Academy, Benjamin West. The Louis XV chairs to the right are part of a furniture bequest by Mrs Desenfans.

2 One of the sketches made by pupils of Soane during the gallery's construction in 1812.

then aware of the College's over-cautiousness in money matters, which was to influence the future building. However, what remains important is that Soane, once he had got hold of an idea, never dropped it. Thus in all his subsequent designs the gallery is understood as part of a future College quadrangle (figs. 8, 27). He continues to remind us of this as late as 1832 when he counters Dibdin's charge against the gallery as 'a graft on the original stock', by pointing out 'that the gallery made only one side of the edifice'.[8] Such dogged persistence was a fundamental trait of Soane's character which was governed by a 'ruling passion . . . to be distinguished as an architect'.[9] He felt this all the more keenly as a self-made man, and it determined his actions at Dulwich.

This became quite obvious after the rejection of his quadrangle project, when his commission was curtailed to a mere reconstruction of the west wing. Instead of settling for a simple rebuilding of the wing on the old site (which indeed had happened in the early eighteenth century with the east wing), he asserts 'that in the Back yard at right angles to [the] present Kitchen would be a more convenient scite [sic]' (figs. 3, 5).[10] This was the very part of the College ground (the garden side) where Soane had envisaged his great quadrangle. Here alone the gallery could still become a focal point of a larger complex. However, with the rebuilding scheme, Soane had to include in his plan lodgings for six almswomen who, as part of the College foundation, had been housed beneath the old gallery.[11] It is unlikely that this provision presented Soane with a serious problem. Indeed, he easily adapted the gallery plan of his original quadrangle design for this new purpose (fig. 6). After two preliminary projects, Soane produced new plans on July 10th, 1811 (fig. 7). They were presented to the Governors on July 12th and after one major amendment, the addition of an east front arcade, were granted approval for 'immediate' execution.

Annoyingly, the ensuing vital part of the building's history remains obscure and we are left to guess what happened. Only two days after the approval we find Soane all of a sudden at home brooding all day over the design.[12] On July 19th new plans, now the final ones, emerge (fig. 8). It could surely be maintained that Soane became alarmed by the increasing financial stinginess of the College and was searching for a plainer version. The effect was startling. It

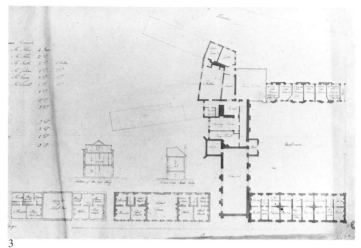

3

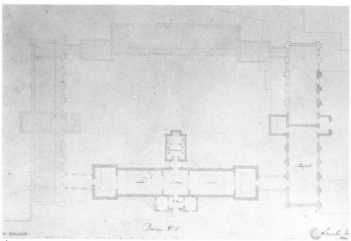

4

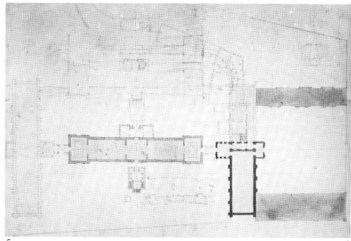

5

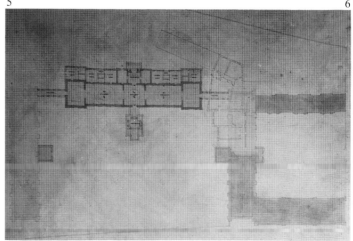

6

3 S——N Blockplan of Edward Alleyn's College of God's Gift (1613–19)
once thought to be designed by Inigo Jones.

4 *First planning stage* 'Design No. 5'. The most important of the five designs submitted May 16th, 1811 for an entirely new College building incorporating only the famous chapel and having the gallery wing as a focal point (for elevations see figs. 13 and 20).

5 *Second planning stage* 'Design No. 6' dated May 1811. Intermediate design for a single gallery after the rejection of the quadrangle project. The rough pencilling above alludes to Soane's next preliminary idea: a first-floor gallery on top of apartments for almswomen (see Drawings List lxv. 4. 39).

6 *Second planning stage* 'Design No. 7', May 25th, 1811. Second preliminary project now with apartments attached to west front (for elevation see fig. 21). Design No. 8, not reproduced here, was similar (see Drawings List lxv. 4. 40).

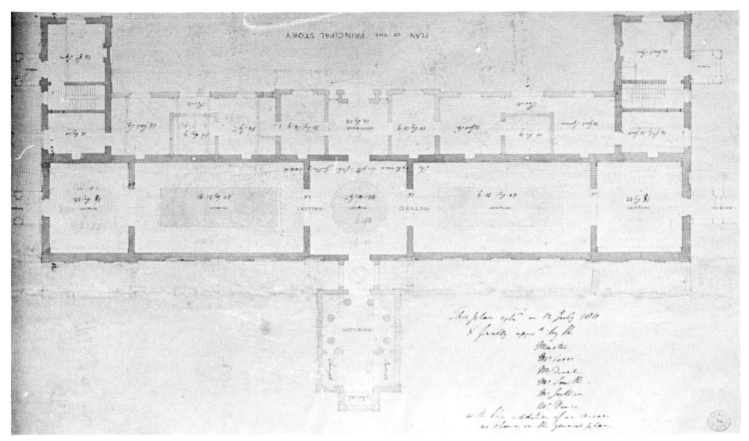

7 *Second planning stage*. The plan approved July 12th, 1811 for 'immediate' execution yet with one amendment: the adding of an east arcade, here pencilled in (for elevation see fig. 22). Note: entrances to the almshouses are still scattered over three fronts.

8 *Second planning stage*. The amended and finally executed design (except for the relocation of the mausoleum) concentrating now all almshouse entrances in the west front creating five instead of three openings with small passages behind as suggested in a design predated by two days (see Drawings List xv. 1. 1).

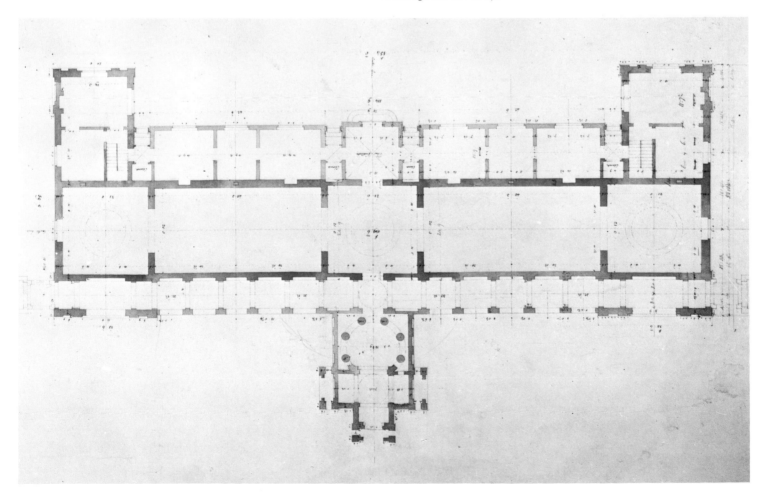

9 Design No. 1, April 17th, 1811, 'Gothic in spirit' with the gallery at the top and the mausoleum next to the chapel in the foreground as required by Bourgeois' will. For other variations to this see Drawings List.

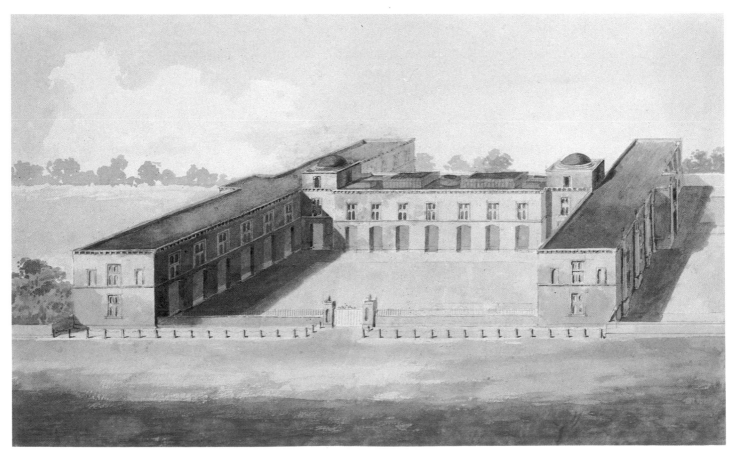

10 Design No. 2, April 17th, 1811. The gallery is the centre of an H-shaped College building indicated by lanterns.

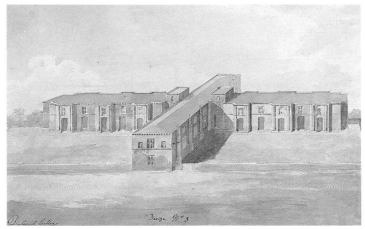

11 Design No. 3, April 1811. A daring yet impracticable suggestion of a cross-shaped building with the gallery most probably on the left.

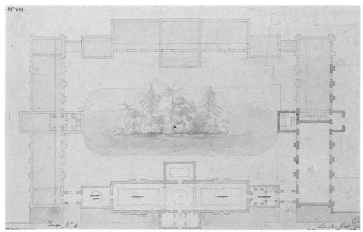

12 Design No. 4, May 1811. The first project to give a clear idea for the arrangement of the gallery, yet with the mausoleum still next to the chapel. Pencil sketches of two elevations both with prominent domed lantern lights seem to belong to this design (see Drawings List lxv. 4. 13 and 29).

13 Design No. 5 of the gallery block, May 1811. The most fully worked out of the quadrangle projects from which the final plan emerged. The false windows would have been Jacobean to correspond with those of the chapel.

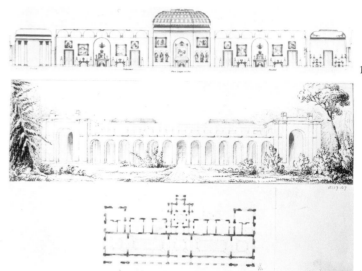

14 Fonthill House Gallery, designed by Soane in 1787. The first top-lit gallery in a country house.

15 The gallery at Castle Howard. C. H. Tatham's design was partly executed

and published in 1811 while Soane was working on the plans for Dulwich.

16 East or entrance front and plan of Dulwich Gallery as built, except for arcade. A descendant of the galleries at Fonthill and Castle Howard.

produced a third stage in his design. As a result of a concentration of the originally scattered almshouse entrances in the principal front, creating five instead of three openings, new elements like the significant small passages are introduced into the plan (figs. 7,8). They called for a substantial remodelling of the exterior, which will be discussed later. Even after the laying of the foundation stone on October 11th, 1811, a major change occurs by moving the mausoleum from the east to the west front. Though easily accomplished, this created a different accent. Once the building was begun with the setting of the stone plinth in April 1812, it progressed rapidly. By September 1812, the shell of the gallery was finished and by the middle of 1813 the interior was ready to receive the pictures which arrived only in 1814.[13] Judging by a note in the *Repository of the Fine Arts*, the gallery was first opened to students of the Royal Academy in 1815.[14]

Dulwich Gallery stands at the very dawn of a century of public museums and galleries. In this it is comparable to Ludwig I's Glyptothek at Munich—the celebrated sculpture gallery designed by Leo von Klenze in 1814–15 and executed in 1816–30. One is also tempted to relate Dulwich to the French Grand Prix designs for museums. Indeed, its interior pattern of two oblong galleries framed and connected by a square room compares with Delannoy's and later Durand's wing composition of their vast museum designs. Yet this French influence is more apparent in English visionary schemes of national museums and galleries popular with a generation of architects younger than Soane, such as Robert Smirke, L. W. Wyatt, J. M. Gandy, Thomas Hardwick and John Foster.[15] Dulwich on the other hand is more to be seen in the English tradition of private galleries. Their history, closely knit to the eighteenth-century country house movement, is far too complex to rehearse here. Their architectural evolution starts with the breaking up of the inherited long gallery. Thus Campbell emphasizes in one of his designs of 1724 that one 'Wing makes one large Gallery ... but the two ends are reduced to Cubes 20ft [as at Dulwich] by introducing some Col-

umns'.[16] Soane himself, when asked in 1787 to design a gallery for the younger Beckford at Fonthill House considered it necessary to divide up the traditional type of long gallery.[17] With pairs of Ionic pilasters and a magnificent alternation of barrel-vaults and domes, he produces a visual break in exactly the ABABA pattern later chosen for Dulwich (fig.14). It is now that the vital change into a functional arrangement of exhibition rooms occurs alongside a transition from private to public viewing. The span between Fonthill and Dulwich is filled by such important galleries as the Shakespeare Gallery (1789) by his teacher Dance (fig. 17), Thomas Hope's Galleries at Duchess Street (1801–04), the Cleveland House Galleries (1795–1806), the Charles Townley Galleries (1800), Leicester's Gallery at No. 24 Hill Street (c.1806) and the Castle Howard Gallery (fig. 15). The last is closest to Dulwich. Incorporated in 1801–12 by C. H. Tatham into Thomas Robinson's Palladian west wing at Castle Howard, it anticipated the plan of Dulwich and furthermore shows a striking similarity in the wide opening arches and curiously coved ceiling (fig.18).[18] In fact, this Palladian inspiration accords well with Soane's views on planning, as expressed in his Royal Academy lectures, where he refers to Palladio's and Scamozzi's proportions 'from square to the double square ... [as] useful and pleasing'.[19] Moreover, Tatham's publication of his plans[20] coincides with the design for Dulwich. Indeed, Soane's earliest elevation with its domed central feature is still very much reminiscent of the gallery wing at Castle Howard.

Unlike all these precedents, Dulwich Gallery is the first to give external expression to the internal function; as such it is unique; as such it is memorable as the first independent gallery building in England.[21] Gradually the gallery evolves out of Soane's original quadrangle; there the basic stylistic and compositional elements are settled. In the first designs two different stylistic versions appear—both an effort to create an harmonious ensemble with the retained chapel, both a tension between classical and Gothic elements, yet neither really successful (figs. 9,13). There is a myth that

17 The Shakespeare Gallery (later British Institution). One of London's most popular exhibition galleries during the late eighteenth and early nineteenth centuries designed by Soane's master George Dance in 1789.

18 Vista through the gallery at Castle Howard showing the ardent art collector, the fifth Earl of Carlisle and his son.

19 Vista through the gallery at Dulwich. Photograph taken c. 1900, still with the original glazing of Soane's lantern.

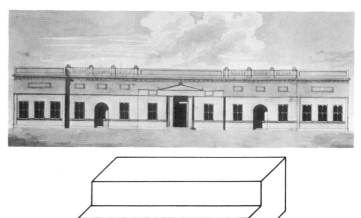

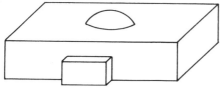

20 The earliest dated design for Dulwich Gallery while still thought of as part of a new College quadrangle: a block-like structure with false Jacobean windows yet clearly bearing Soane's 'own peculiar style', April 4th, 1811 (for plan see fig. 4).

21 Intermediate design of May 1811 after the decision to build merely a gallery wing with lodgings for six almswomen. The latter are simply added on as a low structure on the west front (for plan see fig. 6).

Soane was asked by the College for a Gothic building and that this influenced his first designs.[22] Though there may have been a prevailing anti-classical prejudice, it clearly did not contradict Soane's idiosyncratic style, which after all aims to unite 'not only the potentialities of different kinds of Classic but of Gothic as well'.[23] One could even maintain that Soane felt encouraged by the circumstances to indulge in his very own style. So we have to see the two stylistic versions which he presented as an endeavour to find the right expression within his own stylistic beliefs. The first is one of the barest order, Gothic in spirit, a sincere if uninspired tribute to the Abbé Laugier's anti-ornamental principles (figs. 9–11). The other is based on the classical tradition with a 'Gothic link' to the College (figs. 13,20). Soane's belief in the classical tradition is reflected in his preference for the latter version. It is this which he maintains through different stages, intends for execution and relinquishes only late.

The principal design of the quadrangle stage is a traditional composition, very different from what was eventually executed (fig. 20). It is a heavy block-like structure with a central dome, yet with two bold projections of an entrance

lodge on one side and a mausoleum on the other. However, Soane's advanced primitivist style is clearly indicated by the shaking 'off the trammels of the order' as T. L. Donaldson was later to complain.[24] More surprising is the use of Jacobean sham windows. Though providing the 'Gothic link' to the College, these paradoxically violate Soane's principle that in good architecture 'nothing can be allowed . . . for the introduction of which a good reason cannot be assigned'.[25]

It is the inclusion of the almshouses in this plan which causes a dramatic change and the second stage of the design (fig. 21). The composition only now assumes poetic eloquence with a picturesque variety in heights and projections and a masterly grouping of the masses, which reflect the aesthetic teaching of Price and Knight. Was this the challenge that Soane needed? It is fascinating to imagine the process of invention. Soane seems to carve his composition like a piece of sculpture until a triple arrangement emerges (fig. 22).[26] In a first design, the almshouses are merely added on as a lower projection to the principal (west) front (fig. 21). The more intriguing triple composition appears by a bold projection of the end sections into

25 'Variety in the mass and Light and Shadow in the whole', Soane's final vision of Dulwich Gallery with the mausoleum feature repeated as an entrance porch on the other front. In 1832 Soane still dreamed of completing Dulwich according to this design.[54]

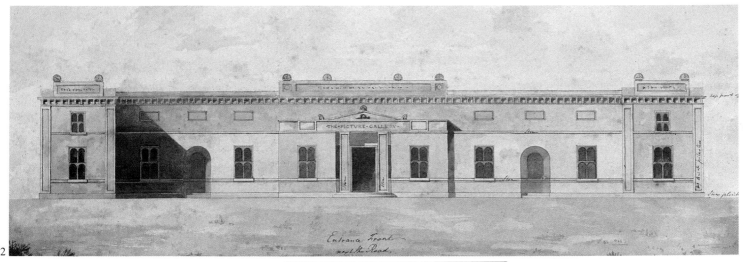

22

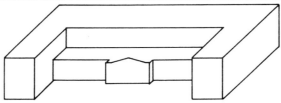

23

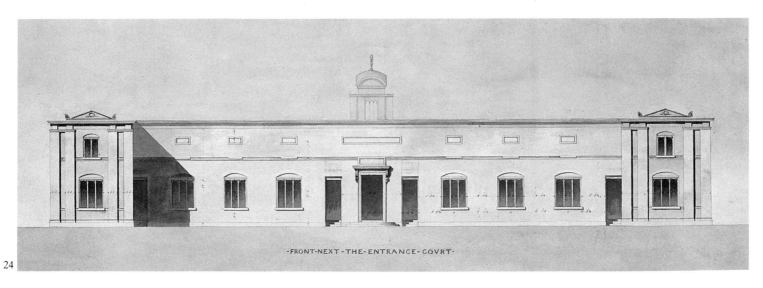

-FRONT-NEXT-THE-ENTRANCE-COVRT-

24

22 West elevation of the plans approved July 12th, 1811 for 'immediate' execution. A triple design with a picturesque grouping, different projections and heights in a slightly more 'Greekified' style.

23 East elevation or mausoleum front of the July 12th plan approved 'with the addition of an arcade' to eliminate the false windows.

24 A simplified, less costly version of the west front, July 29th, 1811. This is one of the designs for the remodelling of the exterior from the third and final planning stage.

26

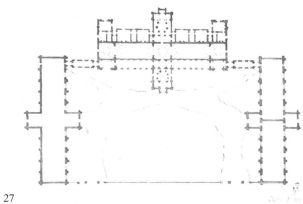

27

28

26 One of Soane's many designs for the 'mausoleum' or east front facing the College garden, July 21st, 1811 (for plan see fig. 8). The arcade on both sides was to connect the gallery to the College buildings.

27 Dulwich Gallery as Soane wished it to be as part of a new College

quadrangle (for elevation see fig. 25). Lithograph plan by C. J. Richardson for Soane's *Designs for Public and Private Buildings*, 1828.

28 Soane's striking new idea for the west front, August 1811. A restless, simplified variant with segmental arches and no emphasis of the entrance.

29 Soane's other idea for the west front with the mausoleum as a dominating feature. A more romantic and classical version than finally executed with pedimented windows set in round arches. Watercolour probably for exhibition at the Royal Academy.

two-storeyed wings framing lower inset apartments with the entrance lodge as a central feature, which is strikingly highlighted in a likewise broken skyline (fig. 22). This is the originally approved plan of July 1811. Yet a stripped version follows abolishing the middle accent of the entrance lodge (fig. 24). Incidentally, it is the shifting of the mausoleum to the front, demanded by Soane in November 1811, which recreates the former elaborate triple design (fig. 25). Can we thus still judge the mausoleum's relocation as an annoying late change contradicting the original intention? Soane himself may have sparked off the idea, as two drawings in the Soane Museum, which considerably pre-date the official decision to relocate the mausoleum, suggest (fig. 33).[27] After all, it is now that Soane considers an accent on both fronts in the form of twin mausolea (one for the entrance), an idea, as Summerson has shown, which derived from Adam's eccentric church at Mistley and which Soane never dropped (figs. 25,27).[28] He had also by now clearly rejected the monotony of the first stage and had reached the climax of his design, fulfilling his innermost belief that 'there must be Order and just Proportion, Intricacy with Simplicity in the component Parts, Variety in the mass, and Light and Shadow in the whole, so as to produce the varied sensations of gaiety and melancholy, of wildness and even of surprise and wonder'.[29]

As a brilliant late thought, the triple arrangement of the west front was echoed on the east 'mausoleum' front in the form of an arcade, which was never, alas, executed.[30] The effect would have been monumental, with two large pylon-like end arches pointing by lower arcades to the climax of the building, the mausoleum. Soane's fondness for this composition with its subtle poetry and dramatic play of light and shadow and its Gothic grace and lightness is documented in many picturesque elevations (fig. 23). It is a sad irony that this solution, which had finally eliminated the painful Jacobean fake windows, showed in its later muti-lated execution a similarly depressing effect with two isolated end arches framing a bleak though arched wall.

The stylistic remodelling came last, forming the third and final stage of the design. Despite the drastic reshaping of the composition, nothing had changed stylistically; the more traditional, classical pattern had been retained becoming even a little more Grecian (at one stage with superb abstract mullions, figs. 20–23). It is the search for a less costly version which provides the change. Soane boldly shifts his design to a plainer stripped version, engrafting his imaginative' individual style (fig. 24). Yet he is not satisfied with such an unsophisticated solution. A more tense, restless variation follows with a typical Soanean dissolution into individual quasi-detached sections mainly achieved by the device of setting the windows into a blind arcade of segmental arches (fig. 28). Here we see Soane in a markedly personal style comparable only to Schinkel's Bauakademie in Berlin. However, the edginess and tension of the segmental arches is again dissolved by finally choosing smoother, round-arched openings, which echo the arcade of the east front (fig. 29). Even so, the building maintains its spare and insistent character with its thin incised lines in the masonry, its stripped pilasters and lid-like cornice, which is heightened by the masterly use of yellow stock brick as the main material and Portland stone for the dressing. Its drastically simplified re-statement of classical themes is striking. Yet a later drawing, presumably for one of the Royal Academy lectures, shows again a more embellished version with a closer link to the classical tradition (fig. 29). Though this may be considered as Soane's actual intention for Dulwich free from any financial restrictions, it can also be seen as proof of the tension of innovation which Britton described as 'a very hazardous point . . . the touchstone of an architect's ability; for it is exceedingly difficult to hit upon the due medium between servility and timidity on the one hand or caprice and rashness on the other.'[31]

The mausoleum was considered by Soane as the most

30 The Mausoleum, Charlotte Street, London, designed by Soane in 1807–08 for the remains of Noel Desenfans, his wife and Sir Francis Bourgeois.

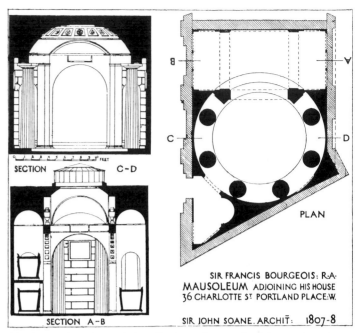

31 Plan and section of the Charlotte Street Mausoleum after A. T. Bolton.

important part of Dulwich. Its combination with a gallery is Soane's unique creation, contradicting Bourgeois' wish to have the mausoleum next to the famous College chapel (fig. 9).[32] It is an immediate and sublime realization of Romanticism's idea of transcendental death. The presence of active pictorial life in the 'brilliantly lighted' gallery is heightened by the awareness of death in the mausoleum with—in Soane's own words—its 'dull religious light ... [showing] the full pride of funeral grandeur ... with the mortal remains of departed worth ... that we almost believe we are conversing with our departed friends'.[33] So the founders are immortalized by the juxtaposition of their lifework with their tombs, by gallery-cum-mausoleum. Soane considered the visitors' circulation between the two spheres as essential—a symbol of the full circle of life—and indeed complained strongly when he later found the door to the mausoleum shut, which was 'destroying its relation to the whole'.[34] Significantly, it is Soane's German counterpart, Friedrich Gilly (1772–1800), who follows the same path with his suggestion of including in his Monument to Frederick the Great (1797) galleries for the King's collection.[35] Soane and Gilly may both have been inspired by the medieval custom of placing founders' graves in churches. The only later example is the Thorvaldsen Museum in Copenhagen which has the artist's tomb in the courtyard.

Bourgeois' wish to reproduce at Dulwich the interior of his private mausoleum in Charlotte Street was faithfully followed by Soane, hence its intimate character (figs. 30,31). Adumbrating a cruciform plan, the main part consists of a square vestibule vaulted by a flattened dome which is supported by a tholos-like arrangement of Greek Doric columns opening abruptly into the sarcophagus chamber, with three bays for the respective tombs of the benefactors.[36] A sunken floor gives the vestibule a crypt-like character, heightened by dramatic lighting effects. Through an invisible lantern with amber-coloured glass, subdued light sheds down on the sarcophagus chamber creating the

'lumière mystérieuse' which Soane so much admired in French churches, and which is intensified by the dim, dark atmosphere of the vestibule (see cover).[37] This novel and striking use of coloured glass, which became a leading feature of Soane's late interiors with their diaphanous lighting effects, was immediately recognized by the prolific architectural topographer John Britton, writing in 1827: 'We ought to thank Mr. Soane ... for showing how it may be applied so as to create many picturesque effects.'[38] However, the mausoleum's effect, with its subtle Greek decoration and sombre Byzantine atmosphere, is more one of exotic simplicity, which appeals to the sensitive mind.

Soane's effort in modelling the mausoleum's exterior is documented in many plans and drawings.[39] The search for its right emphasis in the whole and its subtle integration is his prime consideration. Sometimes it appears as an overpowering central feature with a spire-like lantern, sometimes as a low, insignificant structure, yet always individually emphasized. As with the development of the whole composition, the idea of picturesque grouping emerges late and the mausoleum finally becomes a microcosm of the whole. Its crowning effect is immediately realized by the richer use of Portland stone and the concentration of ornaments (urns, sarcophagi) symbolizing the function. Curiously, it is the controversial late change of plans moving the mausoleum to the west front which results in its intriguing integration, appearing detached yet tightly fitted, squeezed as it is between the almshouses (fig. 43).

The gallery's intimate character, which we cherish so much today, was even more distinct in its original form, then only consisting of the five centre rooms. Yet what appears to us now as an early functional design, the bareness of the rooms enhanced only by lofty separating arches (fig. 34), was in fact dictated by financial restrictions. As such, it compares with the functional and commercially orientated auction and exhibition galleries of the time, such as Spring

32 Another design for the mausoleum's exterior with a saucer dome resembling Soanean ceilings, July 22nd, 1811, a variation of fig. 26. Soane even considered at some stage seated lions at the corners of the lantern (see Drawings List lxv. 4. 45).

33 One of the designs pre-dating the official decision to move the mausoleum to the west front, October 28th, 1811. Note: as in two other designs of this date Soane considers here a different mode of lighting the galleries in the form of high side light (see Drawings List lxv. 4. 35 and 54).

34 1849 lithograph of the interior looking north from the second room. The gallery now appears more formal. None of the furniture (fig. 1) given by Mrs Desenfans is seen any longer except for the Boule clock on a side table at the far end.

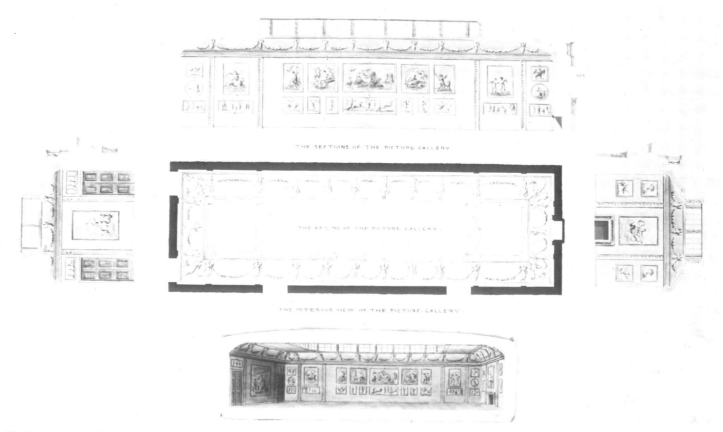

THE SECTIONS OF THE PICTURE GALLERY

THE CEILING OF THE PICTURE GALLERY

THE INTERIOR VIEW OF THE PICTURE GALLERY

35 Soane's design for a picture gallery-cum-museum in the extension to the Senate House, Cambridge, 1791. A far more ornate design than that of Dulwich Gallery yet traditional, and with the same lighting system.

36 Original design for the interior of Dulwich Gallery, May 1811. The intriguing vaulting and lighting system was finally abandoned most probably because of the cost. However, the combination of vertical and sloping lights was realized one hundred years later with the reglazing of the lanterns as may be seen today.

Gardens, Christie's auction galleries in Pall Mall, or the galleries of the British Institution (fig. 17). One has only to look at Soane's delicate interiors and his gallery designs at Fonthill House and Cambridge[40] to imagine what Dulwich might have been (figs. 14,35). There are indeed hints of a more elaborate interior. In one late design, columns are introduced as supports for the arches.[41] Soane also contemplated a more intriguing vaulting system for the galleries with a shallow cupola supported by pendentives and pierced at the top by a glazed lantern (fig. 36). According to Farington, it was the President of the Royal Academy, Benjamin West, who advised Soane in the colour scheme of the gallery. However, Farington strongly condemns it as 'heavy and unfavourable for the pictures, something like burnt oker but heavier'.[42]

Soane certainly needed no advice in the lighting of the gallery. There he could rely on his own experience. In fact, with his Fonthill gallery he had not only created a striking example of a top-lit gallery, but also the first of its kind in an English country house. With the exception of some early skylight rooms at Stourhead (c.1745) and Corsham House (1761–64) and dome light in some of the sculpture galleries, top lighting was then used only in London exhibition and auction rooms because of their desperate need for wall space. However, the impact of Fonthill meant that lighting from above became the universal mode and almost an obligation for every modern gallery—such as at Petworth, Panshanger, Brocklesby and Attingham, to name but a few. Bourgeois himself had his larger paintings exhibited in a sky-lit room at the Charlotte Street house. By the time of Dulwich, the belief in top-lit galleries was such that Britton described them as 'being preferable to any other for a display of works of art'.[43] It seems paradoxical that Fonthill's creation was actually accidental in that Soane had been asked to convert an inner passage on the top floor into a gallery, where top lights could be the only answer. At Dulwich, however, their use was a conscious one, given above all that Soane had briefly considered high side light (fig. 33). He even decided on the rather traditional system of top lantern with vertical glass areas introducing only one single new feature in the form of octagonal rather than rectangular shaped lanterns. This is surprising considering Soane's preoccupation with dome and lantern light. Indeed, in its ingenious and imaginative handling he was rivalled only by his famous contemporary John Nash. Britton points here rightly to 'the many ingenious inventions'[44] in Soane's own house in Lincoln's Inn Fields, where he introduced in his picture gallery a striking combination of clerestory and skylight, a double lantern, where the light, entering in vertical and diagonal rays, is marvellously diffused by a curious pendant arched ceiling. In fact, a similar system was suggested by Soane in his original plan for Dulwich in the form of a circular lantern with vertical and sloping glass areas (figs. 36,38). To prevent overlighting, the cap was filled in, proving Soane's awareness of picture lighting. Even in the final plan he had thought of placing these over the square rooms with oblong lanterns in the larger galleries (fig. 37), which certainly would have created a more pleasing variety than the later formal plan. Yet obviously financial restrictions prevented the execution of this more costly scheme. However, the lighting was strongly criticized at the time. Hazlitt, for example, very harshly remarked that the pictures 'certainly looked better in their old places at the house of Mr. Desenfans . . . the sky-lights are so contrived as to "shed a dim" though not a "religious light" upon them.'[45] A generation later, the Victorian art critic Redgrave likewise complained of poor light in the galleries, leaving no doubt that there were certain imperfections.[46] Yet nowadays none of this seems justified. Soane's still existing lanterns produce quite a satisfactory light which, however, is partly due to their reglazing with sloping glass areas, as Soane had planned for the dome lights.

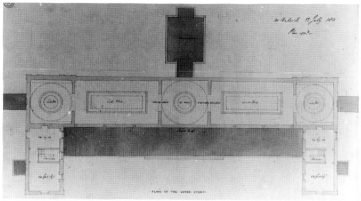

37

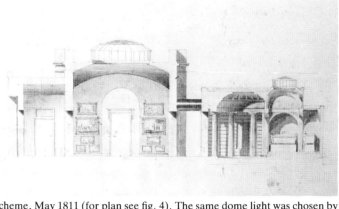

38

37 The pleasing variety of dome and lantern lights as originally planned but replaced in the final scheme by a dull sequence of octagonal lanterns.

38 Section through entrance lobby, gallery and mausoleum of the earliest

scheme, May 1811 (for plan see fig. 4). The same dome light was chosen by Soane for his own house and admired by J. Britton, the architectural topographer, as 'admirably adapted to display pictures and sculptures to advantage'.[55]

The strongest criticism was provoked by the architecture as such. By calling into question the validity of the classical rules, it was only to be expected that Dulwich would incense and confuse its contemporaries (fig. 39). Thus one visitor, The Rev. T. Frognal Dibdin furiously exclaimed: 'What a thing—What a creature it is! A Maeso-Gothic ... Semi-Arabic, Moro-Spanish, Anglico-Norman—a what-you-will production! It hath no compare, there is nothing like it above the earth or under the earth, or about the earth. It hath all the merit and emphatic distinction of being unique.'[47] An article in *Knight's Quarterly Magazine* of 1824 even coined a sixth order, the 'Boetian', to ridicule Soane and his style, ending with a perverse and lengthy ode on 'God's Gift Picture Shop' at Dulwich:[48]

Be theirs the beauties of my style
Myst'ries by none posses'd;—
The roofs unsham'd by slate or tile,
The brick with Portland dress'd,
The *stepless* door, the *scored* wall,
Pillars *sans* base or capital,
And curious antiques;
The chimney-groups that fright the sweep,

And *acroteria* fifty deep,
And all my mighty freaks.

John Britton, Soane's otherwise most dedicated advocate, ignores Dulwich altogether, obviously considering it too daring a subject. For the Victorians, of course, with their belief in architectural copying, Dulwich provided the perfect example, in the words of the architect T. L. Donaldson, '[to] show how dangerous it is for an artist to depart from those examples of the best masters of antiquity'.[49] Fortunately, Soane was already dead when the leading Victorian architectural historian, James Fergusson, proclaimed that 'Soane affected an originality of form and decoration, which, not being based on any well-understood constructive principle, or any recognized form of beauty, had led to no result.'[50] With such sharp criticism, Dulwich naturally was doomed. Indeed, it only once inspired another design, an unexecuted project for the Fitzwilliam Museum, Cambridge by an admirer of Soane, C. H. Tatham (fig. 40).

Yet one criticism Soane need not face is to have failed to provide in his design additional space for future acquisitions. The fact is that Dulwich was created with a single

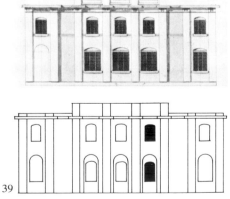

39

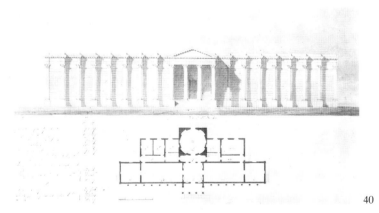

40

39 Design for the north front showing what has been hailed by a contemporary of Soane, R. Brown, as his 'new style of architecture... [with a] peculiar feeling for linear rather than that of foliated decoration'.[56] In the final plan, however, certain modifications are apparent (see below). During the design the window openings constantly changed (see Drawings List lxv. 4. 59–61), and finally all the windows of this front, except for two,

became sham thus preserving the symmetrical composition.

40 An early design for the Fitzwilliam Museum (1827) by an admirer of Soane, C. H. Tatham. The plan is copied from Dulwich Gallery disguised, however, by a facade modelled on a classical precedent, Hadrian's Library at Athens.

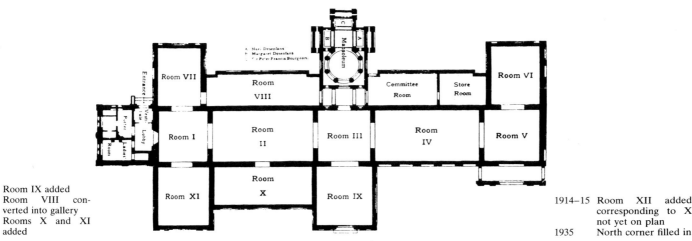

41 The extended gallery in 1914. In 1950–53 a new entrance was made into Room IX and that finally altered the original sense of progression from south to north.

collection in mind and was never regarded as a growing museum institution. Fortunately with the relocation of the almshouses, additional space was gained and accordingly in 1884–85 north and south wings were converted by Charles Barry, junior, the College's architect, into single top-lit galleries. Eighteen years earlier he had built the long-needed entrance lodge, which had been left unexecuted in Soane's design. Added to the south front in a different style and spirit, its destruction in the last war was no loss. By far the largest extension dates from between 1910 and 1915, designed by E. Stanley Hall, who repeated the west rooms of the almshouse side on the east front, yet without finishing the north corner. Two square and two oblong galleries, all lit from above, were thus added (fig. 41). Finally in 1936 H. S. Goodhart-Rendel filled in the north corner. The twentieth-century extension melts so success-fully into the original design that its growth from a single suite of five rooms into a triple row of fourteen rooms, combining galleries and cabinets, is often not realized. It is remarkable how the Edwardian architect Hall paid tribute to Soane at a time when A. T. Bolton, the curator of the Soane Museum, was still considering Dulwich as lacking 'the impressiveness of which Soane's design was capable'.[51]

However, one has to regret that Soane's idea of an entrance arcade is now lost forever due to Hall's gallery addition with its skylights. Goodhart-Rendel's small contribution with its pure Soanean feeling is by far the best. One only hopes that future extensions will maintain this tradition.

Thus it should be remembered that Dulwich is no ordinary work of Soane but his most personal one, for the design of which he charged no fees and for the building of which he was even prepared to pay, when financial difficulties arose (figs. 42,43).[52] Dulwich had provided him with a challenge. Here his friendship with Bourgeois could find expression, here was the ideal rural setting, which he had always considered as the perfect 'scope . . . for the exercise of the talents of the Architect and for displaying the powers of his Art'.[53] These powers developed gradually. In a slow and painstaking process, going through several stages of design, Dulwich finally emerged from an unpretentious early design as one of Soane's most individual expressions in architecture. Though he had to face financial restrictions, these were more of an activating than subduing nature for his imaginative mind. After all, it was this imaginative mind which, as we have seen, initiated and created Dulwich.

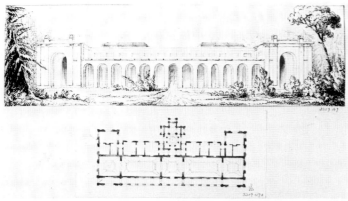

42 The gallery's east front as built except for the arcade, lithograph by C. J. Richardson. It conveys what has been styled by contemporaries as Soane's 'Gothic Feeling', his 'aim to unite the classic delicacies of the Greek and Roman designs with the playfulness of the Gothic, not by the use of the pointed arch, but by adopting the principle'.[56]

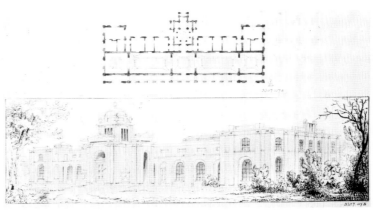

43 West and south front. Richardson's view of the south front is slightly modified showing a windowed facade where actually only two real windows existed.

44 The mausoleum covered with ivy as it was towards the
latter part of the nineteenth century.

NOTES

*For their kind assistance in the preparation of this paper I
am much indebted to Dorothy Stroud, Giles Waterfield, and
Gavin Stamp, and to Mark Stocker, who read the typescript,
and Richard Bosson, who drew the diagrams.*

1 John Summerson, 'Sir John Soane. The Case History of a Personal Style', *RIBA Journal*, 3rd series 58, 1950, p. 88. Soane's personal interest in Dulwich is reflected in several passages of his *Notebooks for the years 1811–1813* (Soane Museum, Transcript Vol. III).

2 J. Soane, *Lectures on Architecture*, ed. A. T. Bolton, 1929, p. 119. Significantly this was written at the time of the erection of the Dulwich Gallery.

3 J. N. G. Sheeran's BA Thesis 'Dulwich College Picture Gallery: A History of the Collection and the Building' is the first with a detailed account of Dulwich. Brief articles are by J. Rykwert, 'The Architecture of Dulwich Picture Gallery', *The Listener*, 71, 1964, pp. 158–59 and G. Teyssot, 'John Soane and the Birth of Style', *Oppositions* 14 (1978), pp. 67–75; the last is partly incorrect. Still the best references for Dulwich are by Sir John Summerson in his various works on Soane.

4 Soane Notebook, Vol. III, December 23rd, 1810.

5 On the history of the old College building, see Arthur Oswald, 'Edward Alleyn's College of God's Gift', *Country Life*, 132, 1962, pp. 1272–74.

6 Reprint of Bourgeois' will in Edward Cook, *Catalogue of the Pictures in the Gallery of Alleyn's College of God's Gift at Dulwich*, London 1914, p. 319.

7 Ed. Wedlake Brayley, *A Topographical History of Surrey*, Vol. III, London 1850, p. 228. See also the better account in Owen Manning and William Bray, *The History and Topography of the County of Surrey*, Vol. 25, London 1847, pp. 433–45. At the time of Bourgeois' bequest £5,800 had already been accumulated for the purpose of rebuilding and restoring.

8 J. Soane, *Designs for Public and Private Buildings*, 2nd edition, London 1832, p. 47.

9 H. M. Colvin, *A Biographical Dictionary of British Architects 1600–1840*, London 1954, p. 559.

10 'Minute for the Private Sittings of the Master, Warden and Fellows of Dulwich College', July 12th, 1811, Dulwich College Library.

11 According to Soane's Design No. 6 (Soane Museum, Dr. lxv. 4. 42) it seems that the almshouses were not immediately included in the project.

12 Soane Notebook, Vol. III, July 14th, 1811.

13 There are twenty-four dated sketches by pupils of Soane recording the different stages of the gallery's erection (Soane Museum, Student Sketchbooks).

14 *Repository of the Fine Arts*, 14, 1815, p. 340. The gallery had already been privately opened in the summer of 1811; the first recorded visit was by Farington on August 31st, 1811, *The Farington Diary*, ed. J. Greig, VII, p. 276.

15 The only still existing plan is Smirke's 'Design for a National Museum', 1799 (British Museum, Print Room). All the others are listed as follows in the *Royal Academy Exhibition Catalogues* (Royal Academy Ar-

45–47 Sketches of Dulwich Picture Gallery made by pupils of Soane during the progress of works, 1812.
6 July 1812.

chives): L. W. Wyatt 'Design for four National Galleries', 1802 (No. 919); J. M. Gandy 'Design of a Gallery', 1803 (No. 927); T. Hardwick 'Design for a National Museum', 1805 (No. 677); J. Foster 'Design for a National Gallery', 1806 (No. 897).

16 *Vitruvius Britannicus*, ed. J. Harris, C3, Pl. 98–99, originally Vol. 3, p.98. Campbell presumably copied his gallery design from the Italian influenced gallery at Wentworth Castle by de Bodt.

17 D. Stroud, *The Architecture of Sir John Soane*, London 1961, p. 33. John Harris, 'Fonthill, Wiltshire I', *Country Life*, 140, 1966, pp. 1370–74.

18 C. Proudfoot and D. Watkin, 'A Pioneer of English Neoclassicism, C. H. Tatham', *Country Life*, 151, 1972, pp. 918–21.

19 J. Soane, *Lectures, op. cit.*, p. 116. In his Lecture No. 7, Soane commits himself at different points to his Palladian background, declaring 'an Edifice to be beautiful must be perfect in its symmetry and uniformity' (p. 113).

20 C. H. Tatham, *The Gallery at Castle Howard*, London 1811.

21 Although G. Dance's superb Shakespeare Gallery is the first building designed for gallery purposes, it was not a free-standing structure but part of Pall Mall's street architecture.

22 Presumably the source for this is L. B. Allen's *Account of the last days of Bourgeois* (partly quoted in Rykwert's article, see note 3). Yet Allen refers here only to the mausoleum, mentioning his personal opinion considering the question of style.

23 J. Summerson, 'Sir John Soane . . .', *op. cit.*, p. 84.

24 T. L. Donaldson, *Review of the Professional Life of Sir John Soane*, 1837, p. 26.

25 J. Soane, *Lectures, op. cit.*, p. 85. Earlier on (p. 45) he says: 'Let us remember the axiom that everything in Architecture is to be accounted for . . . Indeed, this axiom should be as fully impressed on the mind of the student in Architecture, and as much revered as the nose teipsum of the Oracle of Delphos was in ancient time.'

26 Accordingly Soane writes in his Lecture No. 7 (*Lectures, ibid.*, p. 114): 'An edifice can only be considered beautiful when all its parts are in exact Proportion . . . It must form an entire whole from what ever point it is viewed, like a group of Sculpture.'

27 Soane Museum, Dr. lxv. 4. 35 dated Oct. 24, 1811 and Dr. lxv. 4. 18 dated Oct. 28, 1811.

28 There are drawings for this in the Soane Museum (Dr. lxv. 4. 46; Dr. xv. 1. 3) and the V&A Print Room (93 E 19 3307 108 and 3307 111).

29 J. Soane, *Lectures, op. cit.*, p. 114.

30 The motif of an arcade already appears in one of the early quadrangle designs.

31 John Britton, *The Union of Architecture, Sculpture and Painting with descriptive accounts of the house and galleries of John Soane*, London 1827, p. 9 (note 38).

32 Soane Notebook, Vol. III, December 23rd, 1810.

33 J. Soane, *Memoirs of the Professional Life of an Architect*, London 1835, quoted after G. Teyssot (note 3); also in Soane's *Designs for Public and Private Buildings, op. cit.*, p. 48.

34 *Ibid.*

35 Kurt Merckle, *Das Denkmal König Friedrich des Grossen in Berlin. Aktenmässige Geschichte und Beschreibung des Monuments*, Berlin 1894, pp. 65–67.

36 According to Bourgeois' will Margaret Desenfans, the wife of Noel Desenfans, was to be buried in the mausoleum as well.

37 J. Soane, *Lectures, op. cit.*, p. 126.

46 C. Tyrell, 30 July 1812.

38 J. Britton, *The Union of Architecture, Sculpture and Painting*, *op. cit.*, p. 17.

39 The respective drawings are all in the Soane Museum, Dr. lxv. 4.

40 This is an unexecuted design for a gallery-cum-museum as an extension to the Senate House in Cambridge in 1791. Soane Museum, D. lxxii. 3. 12.

41 In a drawing, Soane Museum, Dr. lxv. 4. 60.

42 *The Farington Diary*, *op. cit.*, VII, p. 276.

43 J. Britton, *The Union of Architecture, Sculpture and Painting*, *op. cit.*, p. 18.

44 *Ibid*. Britton refers here to the Bank of England and the design for the new gallery at the House of Lords as displaying 'great imagination and judgement in their domes and lanthorn lights'.

45 W. Hazlitt, *Sketches of the principal Picture Galleries in England*, 1843 edition, p. 23.

46 R. Redgrave, 'Construction of Picture Galleries,' *Builder*, 15, 1857, pp. 689 and 690. Interesting article on contemporary ideas of gallery lighting.

47 Quoted by Soane in his *Designs for Public and Private Buildings*, *op. cit.*, p. 47; furthermore Dibdin remarks 'say what you please, and you cannot say any-thing so delightfully monstrous as is the Exterior in question; and yet we cannot say, "Monstrum- cui lumen *ademptum*" for it has sky-lights in abundance; nor can we pronounce it to be a "faultless monster", such "as the world ne'er saw".'

48 *Knight's Quarterly Magazine*, 1824, pp. 447–63 (461).

49 T. L. Donaldson, *Review of the Professional Life of Sir John Soane*, *op. cit.*, p. 26.

50 James Fergusson, *The History of Modern Architecture*; quoted in Rykwert (note 3), p. 159.

51 A. T. Bolton, *The Architecture and Decoration of R. Adam and Sir John Soane*, London 1920, p. 37.

52 'Minute for the Private Sittings of the Master, Warden and Fellows of Dulwich College', July 12th, 1811, Dulwich College Library. J. N. G. Sheeran (note 3) gives in his thesis on Dulwich a detailed report of all the financial difficulties.

53 J. Soane, *Lectures*, *op. cit.*, p. 114. Anna Jameson later enthusiastically described Dulwich's situation in her *Handbook to Public Galleries* (1842) as 'the Elysian world of shadows' (p. 442).

54 See Soane, *Designs for Public and Private Buildings*, *op. cit.* A watercolour by J. M. Gandy (on open display at the Soane Museum, see Drawings List) refers likewise to this project.

55 In John Britton, *Graphical and Literary Illustrations of Fonthill Abbey*, London 1823, p. 7.

56 In Richard Brown, *Domestic Architecture*, London 1841, p. 289. This is a striking contemporary document for Soane's effect on his fellow architects. Brown, like C. H. Tatham and J. Britton, was an admirer of Soane to whom he pays 'high admiration [for] his taste and talent' regretting that 'he was continually subject to the censure of the poet and the press, and occasionally attacked with much more cruelty than criticism'. However, the highest compliment which Brown pays to Soane, is a design of a 'Museum' in the 'Soanean Style of Architecture' which he includes with detailed drawings.

47 'Gratitude is due to him who strikes out a new path and aspires to perfection, though he may not be able to reach her temple', Sir Joshua Reynolds. Sketch by a pupil of Soane during the progress of works, 1812.

LIST OF DRAWINGS FOR THE DULWICH PICTURE GALLERY ACCORDING TO THE DIFFERENT STAGES OF DESIGN

Key:

SM	In the Soane Museum
lxv.4.1	means Drawer lxv, set 4, drawing 1; key likewise for xv.1.1
*	drawing illustrated here
(I)	Inscription
(d)	date

I DRAWINGS IN THE SOANE MUSEUM

Drawings referring to the 'Old Buildings of Dulwich College'

lxv.4.1 East elevation of west wing with detail of Doric cap and entablature.

lxv.4.2* Ground-floor plan of the old buildings as existing with first- and second-floor plans of the east wing and sections (fig. 3).

lxv.4.3 Elevation, east side of west wing with pilasters similar to those used later for the design of the gallery wing.

lxv.4.4 Plan and section of west wing (d) February 28 1811.

lxv.4.5 Plan of chapel.

First planning stage/Drawings for the gallery as part of a new College quadrangle

lxv.4.6 Design No. 1, block plan. Three-sided quadrangle open to east (d) April 1811.

lxv.4.43 Design No. 1, block plan with walls and open arcade (I) on the left 'Rooms for the persons. appd. to look after the Pictures' (d) 17 April 1811.

lxv.4.7* Design No. 1, bird's-eye view (d) 17 April 1811 (fig. 9).

lxv.4.8 Design No. 1, bird's-eye view, variation (I) 'The Mausoleum placed with the Gallery' (d) May 1811.

lxv.4.9 Design No. 2, block plan (d) April 1811.
Verso: Sketch plan showing the gallery moved back westward.

lxv.4.10* Design No. 2, bird's-eye view (d) 17 April 1811 (fig. 10).

lxv.4.11 Design No. 3, block plan (d) April 1811, cross plan formed by new wings extending north and south from old building.

lxv.4.12* Design No. 3, bird's-eye view (fig. 11).

lxv.4.13* Design No. 4, plan (d) May 1811 (fig. 12).
Verso: Rough pencil sketches of two elevations, both with prominent domed lantern lights. One shows a colonnade (perhaps pilasters only); the other two niches between giant aedicules.

lxv.4.29 Two elevations. Tentative design for the two fronts of the gallery, related to lxv.4.13 *verso* and possibly connected to plan lxv.4.13.

lxv.4.15* Bird's-eye view of a closed-quadrangle design, combining features from Designs No. 4 and No. 5, gallery block referring to plan of Design No. 5 (d) May 1811 (fig. 13).

lxv.4.16* Design No. 5, block plan (d) May 1811 (fig. 4).

lxv.4.28* Elevation of entrance front of gallery. The earliest *dated* design in the collection, (d) April 4th 1811. Same style, paper and size as lxv.4.29 (fig. 20).

lxv.4.30 Elevation of entrance front of gallery. Developed from lxv.4.28, fully dimensioned; the revised attic storey is in Soane's hand (d) 29 April 1811.

lxv.4.17* Interior referring to Design No. 5 (I) 'View of gallery' (d) May 1811 (fig. 36).

lxv.4.14 Interior similar to above lxv.4.17.

Second planning stage/Intermediate designs

lxv.4.42* Design No. 6, plan. Gallery across courtyard; above rough pencilling by Soane shows the gallery set back to form west side of courtyard, two different variations (fig. 5).

lxv.4.39 Plan showing ground floor of gallery block with a central hall, and apartments for old women on either side. The projecting vestibule contains a stair leading to the gallery. Open arcade towards the quadrangle. This plan incorporates revisions proposed in Soane's pencillings on lxv.4.42. Plan probably follows Soane's conference with the Dulwich authorities on May 19th, 1811 when they asked for a plan 'on site of Kitch; and old women undr' (Soane Notebook).

lxv.4.41* Design No. 7, plan (d) 25 May 1811. The apartments for old women are now shown alongside instead of under the gallery as in lxv.4.39 (fig. 6).

lxv.4.20* Design No. 7, elevation of west front of gallery block (fig. 21).

lxv.4.40 Design No. 8, plan. Similar to lxv.4.41 but with the gallery block set further back and quadrant arcades connecting with north and south sides of courtyard.

lxv.4.38 Plan of gallery block as lxv.4.40, but with slight variations.

Second planning stage/Approved plans

lxv.4.37 Block plan (I) 'At Dulwich 12 July 1811' (d) 12 (altered from 10) July 1811 shows gallery as closing block on west side of quadrangle.

lxv.4.34* (I) 'Plan of the Principal Storey' (d) 10 July 1811. Open arcade on west side erased but restored in pencil (I) 'This plan exhd on 12 July 1811 and finally appd by the Master (and 5 other officers) with the addition of an arcade as shown in the general plan' (fig. 7).

lxv.4.33* (I) 'Plan of the Upper Storey' (d) 10 July 1811 (fig. 37).

lxv.4.21* (I) 'Entrance front next the Road' (d) 10 July 1811 (fig. 22).

lxv.4.23* (I) 'Entrance front next the Great Quadrangle' (d) 10 July 1811 (I) 'Section through the lobby between the Mausoleum and the Great Gallery' (I) 'This elevation must be altered to admit the Arcade as settled this 12 July 1811' (fig. 23).

New and final plans emerging 17/19th July 1811

xv.1.1 Plan of the gallery and connecting arcades (d) July 17th 1811, fully dimensioned. The first of the new plans to show such important changes as the concentration of all entrances in west front with small passages behind.

xv.1.2* Plan of the gallery as executed (except for the relocation of the mausoleum and minor variations) (d) 19th July 1811. Substantially revised version of xv.1.1, fully dimensioned (fig. 8).

Third planning stage/The remodelling of the exterior

lxv.4.24 Mausoleum front. Perspective sketch, gallery block from north-east. The earliest exterior representation of the mausoleum but not yet with lantern.

lxv.4.25* Mausoleum front. Perspective sketch by Soane. Gallery from south-east. (I) 'View from the Great Quadrangle of Dulwich showing the proposed design for the Mausoleum of the late Sir Francis Bourgeois and the Gallery to contain the Pictures left by him to Dulwich College' (d) 21 July 1811. Now with prominent lantern with Ionic order (fig. 26).

lxv.4.26* Mausoleum front as in lxv.4.25 but the upper part of the mausoleum has been redesigned without Ionic columns (d) July 22 1811, watercolour (fig. 32).

lxv.4.27 Mausoleum front as in lxv.4.25 and 26 but with modified lantern.

xv.1.4 Two elevations of the gallery.
Above (I) 'Front next the Great Quadrangle' showing the mausoleum.

* *Below* (I) 'Front next the Entrance Court' (d) 29th July 1811 (fig. 24).

xv.2.2 Perspective drawing by J. M. Gandy based on xv.1.4 (I) 'View of a Design for a Mausoleum to the Memory of Sir Francis Bourgeois and a Gallery for the Reception of his Collection of Pictures bequeathed to Dulwich College'. Exhibited RA 1812 (No. 810) watercolour.

Plan and working drawings in August 1811

lxv.4.31 Plan of gallery with north and south wings of quadrangle in outline (d) August 7 1811.

lxv.4.32 Plan of upper part of gallery (d) August 7 1811.

lxv.4.62 Plan of north half of gallery, fully dimensioned.

lxv.4.57 Section through domed centre bay of gallery and mausoleum (showing window in the north wall of the gallery) c. 1811.

* * *

lxv.4.36 Mausoleum front. Perspective sketch from south-east (d) August 8 1811. Similar to lxv.4.24–27 but mausoleum redesigned.

lxv.4.19 Elevation of mausoleum front facing east (d) August 1811.

lxv.4.22* Elevation of entrance front facing west (d) August 1811 (fig. 28).

Drawings for the relocation of the mausoleum, October 1811/Elevations and working drawings 1812

lxv.4.35 Perspective sketch of gallery from north-west with mausoleum towards the road, flanked by old women's apartments (d) October 24th 1811. Long clerestory windows to picture gallery, watercolour.

lxv.4.18* Perspective sketch of gallery from north-west with mausoleum and old women's apartments towards the road, series of three light clerestory windows to picture gallery (d) October 28 1811 (fig. 33).

xv.1.5 Plan of upper part of gallery and elevation towards quadrangle showing unbroken series of 13 arches with series of clerestory windows above, related to lxv.4.18.

lxv.4.54 Elevation of half of entrance front showing slate roof and a series of three light clerestory windows lighting the gallery.

lxv.4.56 (I) 'Elevation of half of the Entrance Front' dimensioned (d) April 13th 1812.

lxv.4.55 Near duplicate to above, dimensioned.

lxv.4.53 (I) 'Elevation of one of the Ends' of the gallery (d) April 1812.

lxv.4.50* Near duplicate to above but reduced in scale (fig. 39).

xv.1.3 Two elevations of the gallery:
Above (I) 'Elevation of the Entrance Front' showing a single-storey vestibule in the style of the mausoleum.
Below (I) 'Elevation of the front next the Road' showing the mausoleum (d) April 13th 1812, watercolour.

lxv.4.63 Outline plan of gallery.

lxv.4.59 Plan of north half of gallery, nearly as executed, fully dimensioned.

lxv.4.60 Plan of north half of gallery showing detached and three-quarter columns in the openings between the galleries, not executed, fully dimensioned.

lxv.4.61 Plan of north half of gallery (I) 'Dulwich College 1811' drawing more probably of 1812. Attached to the bottom proposal for an entrance vestibule of similar size and shape to the mausoleum.

lxv.4.58 Long-section and cross-section through gallery showing lantern lights (d) March 5 1812.

lxv.5.2 Outline plan at high level of half of the gallery block showing flues and detail of a typical chimney stack.

Archive Box b

List N Set XXV Details of chimney tops.

lxv.5.1 Plan of the mausoleum and part of the gallery, horizontal sections.

Designs for the mausoleum

lxv.4.48 Elevation of mausoleum (d) 29 April 1812, dimensioned.
Verso: Variation of mausoleum design.

lxv.4.45 Perspective drawing of mausoleum with seated lions at corners of lantern.

xv.2.7 Perspective view of mausoleum with landscape (d) May 11th 1812, watercolour.

lxv.4.46 Perspective drawing of mausoleum in landscape same aspect as lxv.4.45 with vases at corners of lantern, pinnacled top. Three Roman altars at base. Below this drawing three panels containing miniature sketches of the gallery (d) May 23 1812.

xv.2.5 Perspective view of mausoleum, Roman altars in the angles; sarcophagus and funerary vases within the arch, lantern as erected; in this front also pedimented windows set in round arches as in xv.2.3 and 4, watercolour.

xv.2.6 Perspective view of mausoleum (d) June 11th 1812, watercolour.

lxv.4.44 Elevation of mausoleum, lantern nearly as executed.

lxv.5.3 Elevation of half of the west front of the gallery block, partly as executed; in pencil: pedimented windows with Jacobean lights set in round arches as in xv.2.5.

xv.2.3 Mausoleum and gallery from north-west. Perspective view, probably by J.M. Gandy for RA Exhibition, watercolour.

xv.2.4* Same as above yet lighting and landscape different (fig. 29).

Progress views and plans after 1815 most probably for RA Lectures

Some of these are copies from 'Sketches of the Picture Gallery the Mausoleum and the Sisters Apartments made by the pupils of Sir John Soane during the progress of the works, 1812'. 24 sheets: two by G. Basevi (1/3), five by R. Chantrell (6/14/16/20/21), three by C. Tyrell (10/15/24). SB = Sketchbook.

xv.2.8 Progress view of west front. *Verso:* (I) '12th lect. No 23' copy of SB, watercolour.

lxv.4.47* Progress view, carcass of mausoleum, copy of SB, watercolour.

xv.2.10 Progress view of west front. *Verso:* (I) '12th lect. No 24' copy of SB, watercolour.

xv.2.9 Progress view of interior. *Verso:* (I) '12th lect. No 25' copy of SB, watercolour.

xv.2.11 Progress view of west front, copy of SB, watercolour.

lxv.4.49 Plan of gallery with dimensions taken from lxv.4.59, probably part of a record set made after 1815.

lxv.4.51 Elevation of west front on paper with WM 1815 showing a former scheme with three pane rectangular windows set in segmental arches as in lxv.4.22.

lxv.4.52 Elevation of east front, relating to above.

Watercolour on open display in the Soane Museum
by J. M. Gandy. Exhibited RA 1823 (No. 1056).
Drawing divided into nine panels
(I) 'DULWICH COLLEGE. The Picture Gallery and the MAUSOLEUM erected pursuant to the WILL and at the expense of the late SIR FRANCIS BOURGEOIS'.
(I) 'This assemblage has been made to illustrate the doctrine of the Rev. T. F. Dibdin lately propagated respecting the advantages to the Public of liberal criticism and the unshackled freedom of the Press'.

Top left	(I) 'Angular view from the Entrance Court agreeably to the original design'.
*Left centre**	(I) 'The Picture Gallery' (fig. 1).
Bottom left	(I) 'The plan of the building in its present unfinished and altered state'.
Top centre	(I) 'View of the Entrance Front in its present unfinished state'.
Centre	(I) 'Central view from the Entrance Court agreeably to the original design'.
Bottom centre	(I) 'View of the Lawn front of the building with the omission of the temporary entrance at the South east corner'.
Centre right	(I) 'The Mausoleum'.
Bottom right	(I) 'The plan of the building agreeably to the original design'.

II DRAWINGS IN THE VICTORIA AND ALBERT MUSEUM, PRINTS AND DRAWINGS DEPARTMENT
There is a volume with a collection of drawings by Sir John Soane and C. J. Richardson 93 E 18–19. Pages 119–135 refer to Dulwich and the mausoleum in Charlotte Street with the Richardson originals for the Dulwich Lithographs in Soane's *Designs for Public and Private Buildings*, 1828. Also:

93 E 18/3306 176 Elevation of gallery block (I) 'Dulwich College' exactly like SM lxv.4.28.

93 E 19/3307 108* Perspective view of gallery from north-east (fig. 25).

93 E 19/3307 109* Section through entrance lobby, gallery and mausoleum of the earliest scheme relating to SM lxv.4.16 and 28 (fig. 38).

*   *   *

TABLE OF COSTS FOR THE CONSTRUCTION OF THE DULWICH PICTURE GALLERY

1st estimate given by Soane to Mr. Allen, May 16th, 1811 .... £ 8,000
2nd estimate given by Soane to Mr. Allen, July 12th, 1811.......... £11,270
Actual Cost...£9,788 14s 11d

		£	s	d
BRICKLAYING	(J. & H. Lee).....................	2,804	3	3
CARPENTRY	(Martyr & Son)....................	2,343	7	2¼
"	(H. Tristam) May 8th, 1812– April 23rd, 1814	589	5	2½
"	(" ") May 14th, 1814– July 1st, 1814.....	0	15	7½
MASONRY	(Thomas Grundy)................	1,243	6	6¼
"	(John Day & Son)...............	553	9	5
PLASTERING	(John & Joshua Bayley)	392	5	10¾
"	(William Rothwell).............	1	2	6
PLUMBING	(William Good)	777	16	3¾
"	(Lancelot Burton)	385	14	3½
PRINTING & GLAZING	(William Watson)	373	3	2
SMITHING	(Thomas Russell)	49	18	2
"	(James Mackell & Co.)	21	2	4
"	(Thomas Hearsey)...............	9	9	0
SLATING	(W. & J. Sharp)	39	13	1½
METAL SASHES	(Underwood & Doyle)	46	3	8
IRON MONGERY	(Stevens, Wedd & Co.).........	13	7	6
WORKMEN'S DINNER	....	24	14	9
CLERK OF THE WORKS	(Henry Harrison)	40	19	0
	(James Cook)	68	8	0
	(Walter Payne)	10	10	0
	TOTAL	£9,788	14	11

Design for a Canine Residence, Rome 1779. Redrawn by C. J. Richardson, c. 1835. (Dr. xiv. 4. 2)

Cumberland Gate, Hyde Park, 1797. Drawing by J. M. Gandy. (Fo. v. 178)

Pelwall House, Staffordshire, 1821. Entrance Front. (Fo. vi. 4)

Design for the monument to Mrs Soane in the graveyard of St Giles-in-the-Fields (now St Pancras Gardens), 1816. (Dr. xiv. 4. 8)

List of Buildings

The following listing is based on the entry in Howard Colvin's *A Biographical Dictionary of British Architects 1600–1840* (1978 edition), published by John Murray, which should be consulted for bibliographical references.

COUNTRY HOUSES, ETC.

PETERSHAM LODGE, SURREY, repairs and decorations for Thomas Pitt, later 1st Lord Camelford, 1781–2; demolished *c.* 1835.

WALTHAMSTOW, ESSEX, new room for James Neave, 1781, perhaps at CLEVELANDS, demolished 1960.

HAMELS (now Crofton Grange), nr. BUNTINGFORD, HERTFORDSHIRE, alterations, entrance lodges and dairy for the Hon. Philip Yorke, 1781–3; remodelled c. 1830–40.

COOMBE HOUSE, nr. KINGSTON, SURREY, repairs and alterations for the Hon. Wilbraham Tollemache, 1782–5; demolished 1933.

BURN HALL, COUNTY DURHAM, Neoclassical cow-house for George Smith, 1783.

WALTHAMSTOW RECTORY MANOR, ESSEX, enlarged for William Cooke, 1783–4; demolished. c. 1897.

BURNHAM WESTGATE HALL, NORFOLK, alterations and additions for Thomas Pitt, later 1st Lord Camelford, 1783–5.

TYTTENHANGER, HERTFORDSHIRE, repairs for the Hon. Mrs. Yorke, 1783 and 1789.

MALVERN HALL, SOLIHULL, WARWICKSHIRE, added wings, etc., for Henry Greswold Lewis, 1783–6; wings demolished 1899.

LETTON HALL, NORFOLK, for B. G. Dillingham 1783–9.

SAXLINGHAM RECTORY, NORFOLK, for the Rev. J. Gooch, 1784–7.

COSTESSY HALL, NORFOLK, stable and dovecote for Sir William Jerningham, Bart., 1784; probably built but demolished.

TAVERHAM HALL, NORFOLK, alterations for M. S. Branthwayt, 1784–8; rebuilt by D. Brandon, 1858–9.

EARSHAM HALL, nr. BUNGAY, NORFOLK, Music Room for William Wyndham, 1784–5.

TENDRING HALL, SUFFOLK, for Sir Joshua Rowley, Bart., 1784–6; demolished 1955.

LANGLEY PARK, NORFOLK, two sets of lodges for Sir Thomas Beauchamp-Proctor, Bart., 1784 onwards.

SHOTESHAM PARK, NORFOLK, for R. Fellowes, 1785–8.

BLUNDESTON HOUSE, SUFFOLK, for Nathaniel Rix, 1785–6.

CHILLINGTON HALL, STAFFORDSHIRE, remodelled for Thomas Giffard, 1785–9. There are drawings by Soane in the William Salt Library at Stafford: 'Staffordshire Views' iii, ff. 95–107.

PIERCEFIELD, nr. CHEPSTOW, MONMOUTHSHIRE, rebuilt for George Smith, 1785–93; now in ruins.

LEES COURT, KENT, alterations to house and new stables for L. T. Watson, 1786.

CRICKET LODGE, CRICKET ST. THOMAS, SOMERSET, alterations and additions for Admiral Hood, 1st Viscount Bridport, 1786 and 1801–4; since much altered.

RYSTON HALL, NORFOLK, remodelled for Edward Pratt, 1786–8.

BOCONNOC, CORNWALL, repairs for the 1st Lord Camelford, 1786–88.

MULGRAVE HALL, YORKSHIRE (N.R.), alterations and additions for the 2nd Lord Mulgrave, 1786; remodelled by William Atkinson as Mulgrave Castle, c. 1804–11.

HOCKERILL, nr. BISHOP'S STORTFORD, HERTFORDSHIRE, house for R. Winter, 1786.

BEAUPORT, nr. BATTLE, SUSSEX, designs for greenhouse and obelisk for General the Hon. James Murray, 1786 and 1790; house demolished 1923.

NACKINGTON HOUSE, KENT, alterations for R. Milles, 1786; demolished.

HOLWOOD HOUSE, KENT, alterations and additions for William Pitt, 1786 and 1797–8; demolished 1823.

SKELTON CASTLE, YORKSHIRE (N.R.), alterations and additions, including stables, for John Hall (later Wharton), 1787.

FONTHILL HOUSE, WILTSHIRE, picture gallery for Alderman William Beckford, 1787; demolished 1807.

HETHERSETT, NORFOLK, design for house for J. F. Iselin, 1788.

KELSHALL RECTORY, HERTFORDSHIRE, designs for alterations for the Rev. Thomas Waddington, 1788.

BENTLEY PRIORY, STANMORE, MIDDLESEX, alterations and additions for the 1st Marquess of Abercorn, 1788–98; enlarged by R. Smirke 1810–18; subsequently much altered.

Saxlingham Rectory, 1784–87.

Shotesham Park, 1785–88.

WARDOUR CASTLE, WILTSHIRE, enlarged CHAPEL (R.C.) for the 8th Lord Arundell of Wardour, 1788.

BEMERTON RECTORY, WILTSHIRE, designs for alterations for Dr. William Coxe, 1788.

RICHMOND PARK, SURREY, HILL or PEMBROKE LODGE, alterations for the Countess of Pembroke, 1788 and 1796.

GAWDY HALL, nr. HARLESTON, NORFOLK, alterations for the Rev. Gervase Holmes, 1788; demolished 1939.

WOKEFIELD PARK, BERKSHIRE, alterations and new gateway for Mrs. Brocas, 1788–9; altered c. 1845.

SYDNEY LODGE, HAMBLE, HAMPSHIRE, for the Hon. Mrs. Yorke, 1789.

TAWSTOCK COURT, DEVON, alterations to exterior (castellated) and new staircase for Sir Bourchier Wrey, Bart., 1789.

WRETHAM HALL, NORFOLK, for William Colhoun, 1789; rebuilt in nineteenth century; demolished. c. 1905.

FAIRFORD PARK, GLOUCESTERSHIRE, alterations for J. R. Barker, 1789; demolished c. 1960.

GUNTHORPE HALL, NORFOLK, for Charles Collyer, 1789; altered 1880 and 1900.

HALSNEAD HALL, WHISTON, LANCASHIRE, south front for Richard Willis, 1789; demolished 1932.

CHILTON LODGE, nr. HUNGERFORD, BERKSHIRE, for William Morland, 1789–90; rebuilt by W. Pilkington 1800.

WOODEATON MANOR, OXFORDSHIRE, new porch and kitchen wing for John Weyland, 1790.

COLNE PARK, ESSEX, Ionic column in park for Philip Hills, 1790.

WILLIAMSTRIP PARK, GLOUCESTERSHIRE, refitted library for Michael Hicks Beach, 1791; altered c. 1940.

WISTON HALL, WISSINGTON, SUFFOLK, for Samuel Beachcroft, 1791.

WHICHCOTES, HENDON, MIDDLESEX, repairs for John Cornwall, 1791.

NETHERAVON HOUSE, WILTSHIRE, enlarged for Michael Hicks Beach, 1791; since much altered.

BARON'S COURT, COUNTY TYRONE, IRELAND, additions for the 1st Marquess of Abercorn, 1791–2; rebuilt in nineteenth century.

WIMPOLE HALL, CAMBRIDGESHIRE, alterations and additions, including Yellow Drawing Room and Book Room, for the 3rd Earl of Hardwicke, 1791–3.

TAPLOW, BUCKINGHAMSHIRE, additions to house for Lady Wynn, 1792.

SULBY HALL, NORTHAMPTONSHIRE, for René Payne, 1792–5; apparently remodelled c. 1830; demolished c. 1953 [stated to be by Soane in J. P. Neale, *Views of Seats*, 1st ser., vi, 1823, and confirmed by Soane's ledgers].

TYRINGHAM HALL, BUCKINGHAMSHIRE, including lodge and bridge, for William Praed, 1793–c. 1800; interior altered, dome a modern addition.

SOUTHGATE, MIDDLESEX, alterations to house for Thomas Lewis, 1793.

CAIRNESS HOUSE, ABERDEENSHIRE, completion, 1794–7, of house designed by James Playfair for Charles Gordon.

CUFFNELLS, nr. LYNDHURST, HAMPSHIRE, south front, etc., for George Rose, 1794–5; demolished c. 1950.

PITSHILL, nr. TILLINGTON, SUSSEX, designs for north front for William Mitford, executed in modified form, 1794.

SUNBURY PLACE, MIDDLESEX, designs for alterations for Roger Boehm, 1794.

SOUTHGATE, MIDDLESEX, alterations to house at Palmer's Green for Samuel Boddington, 1795.

BAGDEN or SAVERNAKE LODGE, SAVERNAKE FOREST, WILTSHIRE, enlarged for the 1st Earl of Ailesbury as a residence for his son Lord Bruce, 1795; destroyed by fire 1861.

WESTON, nr. SOUTHAMPTON, HAMPSHIRE, alterations for W. Moffat 1797; demolished. Although Soane was responsible for alterations to this house in 1797, subsequent references in Soane's journal suggest that he may have been superseded by Willey Reveley.

NORTH MIMMS PARK, HERTFORDSHIRE, repairs and new dairy and greenhouse, etc., for the 5th Duke of Leeds, 1797.

CLAPHAM, WANDSWORTH, SURREY, alterations to house for T. A. Green, 1798.

BAGSHOT PARK, SURREY, alterations for the Duke of Clarence, 1798; demolished.

BETCHWORTH CASTLE, SURREY, alterations to house and new stables, etc., for Henry Peters, 1798–9.

HEATHFIELD LODGE, ACTON, MIDDLESEX, alterations for John Winter, 1798.

RICHMOND PARK, SURREY, THATCHED HOUSED LODGE, alterations to dining-room, etc., for General Sir Charles Stuart, 1798.

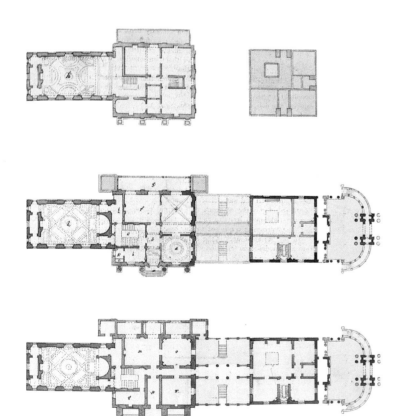

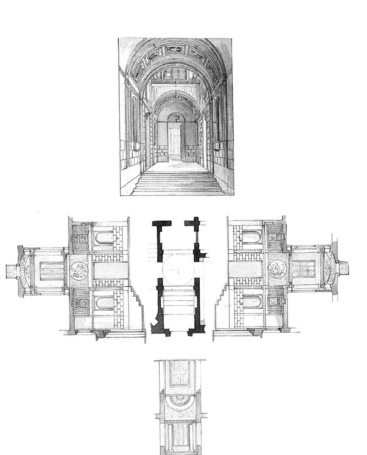

Pitzhanger Manor, Ealing, 1800–03. *Above* (clockwise): entrance front, garden front, rustic bridge, gateway. *Below left*: basement, ground- and upper-floor plans; *right*: plan, sections and view of the entrance hall.

Sketches by C. J. Richardson for illustrations in the *Memoirs*, 1835. (Sc. shelf B)

The State Paper Office, St James's Park, built in 1830. *Left*: Main entrance. *Right*: Detail of triple window. *Below*: Side elevation. Drawings by George Bailey.

Tyringham Hall and bridge, 1793–c. 1800.

DOWN AMPNEY HOUSE, GLOUCESTERSHIRE, alterations for the Hon. John Eliot, 1799.

AYNHO PARK, NORTHAMPTONSHIRE, remodelled interior and altered exterior for W. R. Cartwright, 1799–1804.

ALBURY PARK, SURREY, north front and internal alterations for Samuel Thornton, 1800–2; exterior remodelled by A. W. & E. W. Pugin 1842 onwards.

PITZHANGER PLACE or MANOR, EALING, MIDDLESEX (now Public Library), largely rebuilt for himself, 1800–2.

RICKMANSWORTH, HERTFORDSHIRE., THE MOAT HOUSE, designs for alterations and additions for T. H. Earle, 1800.

SOUTH HILL PARK, BRACKNELL, BERKSHIRE, alterations for George Canning, 1801.

NORWOOD GREEN, MIDDLESEX, house for John Robins, 1801; demolished.

COOMBE HOUSE, nr. KINGSTON, SURREY, alterations, including library, for Lord Hawkesbury, later 2nd Earl of Liverpool, 1801; demolished 1933.

GREENWICH, KENT, MACARTNEY HOUSE, alterations for the Hon. G. F. Lyttelton, 1802.

LITTLE HILL COURT, HERTFORDSHIRE, designs for alterations for Mrs. Saunders, 1803.

HAMPSTEAD, LONDON, new entrance and other alterations to house for Daniel Bayley, 1803.

PORT ELIOT, ST. GERMAN'S, CORNWALL, remodelled house and designed new stables for the 2nd Lord Eliot, 1804–6, castellated; entrance hall and porch by H. Harrison 1829.

RAMSEY ABBEY, HUNTINGDONSHIRE, remodelled for H. Fellowes, 1804–7; remodelled by E. Blore 1838–9.

ROEHAMPTON, SURREY, CEDAR COURT, enlarged for John Thomson, 1804–7; demolished 1910–13.

STOWE HOUSE, BUCKINGHAMSHIRE, Gothic library for the 1st Marquis of Buckingham, 1805–6.

ASTROP PARK, NORTHAMPTONSHIRE, additions for the Rev. W. S. Willes, 1805; reduced in size 1961.

ENGLEFIELD HOUSE, BERKSHIRE, repairs for Richard Benyon, 1806 [drawings in Berkshire County Record Office, D/EBY 23 and C14].

WHITLEY ABBEY, WARWICKSHIRE, alterations for the 1st Viscount Hood, 1810; demolished 1953.

MOGGERHANGER HOUSE, BEDFORDSHIRE, rebuilt for Stephen Thornton, 1809–11.

MELLS PARK, SOMERSET, alterations, including entrance and library, for Col. Thomas Horner, 1810–24; demolished after fire in 1917.

EVERTON HOUSE, BEDFORDSHIRE, alterations for William Astell, 1811–2; demolished.

WALMER COTTAGE, KENT, additions for Capt. Lee, 1812.

RINGWOULD HOUSE, KENT, for the Rev. John Monins, 1813.

BUTTERTON, STAFFORDSHIRE, BUTTERTON GRANGE FARMHOUSE,

Pitzhanger Manor, 1800–02.

Aynho Park, 1799–1804.

Moggerhanger House, 1809–11.

for Thomas Swinnerton, 1815.

MARDEN HILL, TEWIN, HERTFORDSHIRE, new porch and other alterations for C. G. Thornton, 1818–19.

WOTTON HOUSE, BUCKINGHAMSHIRE, reconstructed interior after fire for the 2nd Marquis of Buckingham, 1821–2.

PELLWALL HOUSE, nr. MARKET DRAYTON, STAFFORDSHIRE, for Purney Sillitoe, 1822–8.

HARDENHUISH HOUSE, WILTSHIRE, alterations and additions for Thomas Clutterbuck, 1829.

LONDON HOUSES, ETC.

PICCADILLY, NO. 148, completion and decoration for the Hon. Wilbraham Tollemache, 1781–8.

ADAMS PLACE, SOUTHWARK, shops and tenements for Francis Adams, 1781–4; demolished.

BERKELEY SQUARE, alterations for the Hon. Mrs. Perry, 1782–3.

NEW CAVENDISH STREET, NO. 63 (formerly NO. 1), alterations for the Hon. P. Yorke, 1782–4.

WIMPOLE STREET, repairs to house for Sir John Stuart of Allanbank, 1783.

SAVILE ROW, NO. 18, alterations to drawing-room for Lady Banks, 1784.

PALL MALL, NO. 103, shop-front for Mr. Crooke, 1790; demolished 1836–7.

HILL STREET, NO. 23, alterations for the 1st Earl Fortescue, 1791.

PALL MALL, NO. 56, alterations for Messrs. Ransom, Morland & Hammersley, 1791.

PHILPOT LANE, NO. 15, repairs and decorations for Peter Thellusson, 1792.

FENCHURCH STREET, NO. 27, repairs and decorations for Charles Thellusson, 1792.

MARK LANE, NO. 17, repairs and alterations for Samuel Boddington, 1792.

UPPER GROSVENOR STREET, NO. 1, repairs for Mrs. Brocas, 1792 and 1819.

BUCKINGHAM HOUSE, NO. 91 PALL MALL, rebuilt for the 1st Marquis of Buckingham, 1792–5; further alterations and repairs 1813–14; demolished 1908.

LINCOLN'S INN FIELDS, NO. 12, for himself, 1792–4.

PALL MALL, NO. 104, alterations for Lady Louisa Manners, 1793–4; demolished c. 1837.

LINCOLN'S INN FIELDS, NO. 51, alterations for John Pearse, 1794; demolished 1904.

STRATTON STREET, NO. 12, for Col. Thomas Graham, 1795–7.

SOUTH AUDLEY STREET, NO. 56, repairs and decorations for

New Bank Buildings, 1807–10.

10 Downing Street, 1825–26.

The Court of Exchequer, Westminster, 1826.
Drawing by J. M. Gandy. (Fo. vi. 55)

The Court of King's Bench, Westminster, 1826.
Drawing by J. M. Gandy. (Fo. vi. 43)

The Court of Chancery, Westminster, 1823. Drawing by J. M. Gandy. (N. Drg. Rm.)

Privy Council Chamber, Downing Street, 1824–27. (Dr. xv. 5. 1)

Blackfriars Bridge, 1783–84. (Pfl. iii. 9)

The Bank of England, 1788–1833.

Miss Anguish, 1795.

LINCOLN'S INN FIELDS, NOS. 57–8, divided into two houses, with new porch, 1795

PORTLAND PLACE, NO. 35 (now 70), repairs and alterations for Sir Alan, later 1st Lord Gardner, 1795 and 1810.

ST. JAMES'S SQUARE, NO. 21, completion of house designed by R. F. Brettingham for the 5th Duke of Leeds, 1795; demolished 1934.

PARK LANE, alterations and repairs to house for the 2nd Earl of Mornington, 1796.

LOWER GOWER STREET, NO. 34, alterations for Mrs. Peters, 1798.

ST. JAMES'S SQUARE, NO. 22, internal alterations for Samuel Thornton, 1799, and repairs, 1805 and 1811; demolished 1847.

MANSFIELD STREET, NO. 12, alterations for Charles Mills, 1799.

GEORGE STREET, HANOVER SQUARE, NO. 24, alterations for Dr. Pemberton, 1799.

GROSVENOR SQUARE, NO. 22 (later 25), alterations for the 1st Marquess of Abercorn, 1799.

OLD BOND STREET, CITY, alterations for Stephen Thornton, 1800.

PARK STREET, MAYFAIR, NO. 50 or 51, repairs for Henry Peters, 1800.

NEW NORFOLK (NOW DUNRAVEN) STREET, NO. 22, alterations for J. Hammet, 1801, completed by James Spiller.

FLEET STREET, NO. 189, Bank for William Praed, 1801; demolished 1923.

FOUNTAIN COURT, ALDERMANBURY, new premises for W. A. Jackson, Peters & Co., 1802; demolished.

GROSVENOR SQUARE, NO. 44, alterations for Robert Knight, 1802; demolished.

PARK LANE, alterations to windows of house for the 4th Earl of Breadalbane, 1803.

UPPER GROSVENOR STREET, NO. 14, alterations for Thomas Raikes, 1803.

CURZON STREET, NO. 19, alterations for Sir John Sebright, Bart., 1803.

ST. JAMES'S SQUARE, NO. 33, alterations for the 2nd Lord Eliot, 1805–7.

SOUTH AUDLEY STREET, NO. 6, decorations for Richard Benyon, 1805.

FREDERICK'S PLACE, NO. 4, alterations for Thomas Lewis, 1806.

DEAN STREET, MAYFAIR, alterations for Mr. Knight, 1807.

NEW BANK BUILDINGS, PRINCES STREET, LOTHBURY, 1807–10; demolished 1891.

GROSVENOR SQUARE, NO. 34, alterations for Mrs. Benyon, 1807.

Chelsea Hospital, 1809–17. (Dr. xiv. 7. 2)

Dulwich Picture Gallery, 1811–14.

CHARLOTTE (NOW HALLAM) STREET, NO. 38, mausoleum for Sir Francis Bourgeois, 1807; demolished.

WHITEHALL, FIFE HOUSE, repairs and alterations for the 2nd Earl of Liverpool, 1809; demolished.

PARK LANE, NO. 22 (later 18,) for John Robins, 1812.

LINCOLN'S INN FIELDS, NO. 13, for himself, 1812–13.

WHITEHALL, CARRINGTON HOUSE, stables and minor alterations to house for the 1st Lord Carrington, 1816–18; demolished 1886.

GROSVENOR SQUARE, NO. 13, alterations for the 2nd Lord Berwick, 1816.

ST. ALBAN'S STREET, ST. JAMES'S, stabling for the 1st Earl of St. Germans, 1816–18; demolished.

THREADNEEDLE STREET, NO. 62, alterations to Bank for Grote, Prescott & Grote, 1818.

ST. JAMES'S SQUARE, NO. 3, alterations and additions for the 4th earl of Hardwicke, 1818–19; demolished 1930.

MONTAGUE PLACE, BLOOMSBURY, NO. 16, alterations for Henry Hase, 1820.

REGENT STREET, NOS. 156–172 on east side, houses and shops for J. Robins and others, 1820–1; demolished.

LINCOLN'S INN FIELDS, NO. 14, for himself, 1823–4.

DOWNING, STREET, NOS. 10–11, internal alterations, 1825–6.

BELGRAVE PLACE, NO. 30, ante-room to sculpture gallery for Sir Francis Chantrey, 1830–1; demolished.

PUBLIC BUILDINGS, ETC.

NORWICH, BLACKFRIARS BRIDGE (River Wensum), 1783–4; since widened.

WALTHAMSTOW CHURCH, ESSEX, alterations, 1784.

NAYLAND CHURCH, SUFFOLK, pewing, etc., 1785.

HINGHAM CHURCH, NORFOLK, alterations to chancel, including Gothic reredos since removed, 1785.

LONDON, THE BANK OF ENGLAND, rebuilt 1788–1833; rebuilt 1930–40.

NORWICH CASTLE, rebuilt COUNTY GAOL, 1789–94, castellated; demolished 1825.

CAMBRIDGE, CAIUS COLLEGE, remodelled interior of Hall, 1792; converted into rooms 1853.

LONDON, HYDE PARK, CUMBERLAND GATE and lodge, 1797; demolished.

LONDON, CONSTITUTION HILL, lodge and gateway, 1797.

BRAMLEY CHURCH, HAMPSHIRE, added BROCAS CHAPEL for Mrs. Brocas, 1802, Gothic.

WAKEFIELD, ALL SAINTS CHURCH (now Cathedral), report on repair of spire.

READING, BERKSHIRE, obelisk in Market Place for Edward Simeon, 1804.

OXFORD, BRASENOSE COLLEGE, converted cloister into rooms, 1807.

The House of Lords, 1822–27.

St Peter's Church, 1823–24.

Designs presented to the Commissioners for New Churches. Drawing by J. M. Gandy, 1825. (Dr. xv. 4. 8)

Design for a model church. Drawing by J. M. Gandy, c. 1825. (Dr. xv. 4. 6)

Holy Trinity Church, 1826–27.

BELFAST, IRELAND, THE ACADEMICAL INSTITUTION, COLLEGE SQUARE, 1809–14, representing a much simplified version of his original designs.

CHELSEA HOSPITAL, LONDON, the INFIRMARY, STABLES and additions to Clerk of the Works' House, 1809–17. The house was demolished 1858 and the Infirmary was destroyed by bombing in 1941.

DULWICH COLLEGE, THE PICTURE GALLERY and MAUSOLEUM, 1811–14; restored after bomb damage in 1944.

LONDON, THE NATIONAL DEBT REDEMPTION AND LIFE ANNUITIES OFFICE, OLD JEWRY, 1818–19; demolished c. 1900.

WESTMINSTER, THE LAW COURTS, 1822–5; demolished 1883. The exterior was Gothicized against Soane's wishes, in accordance with a design which he disowned.

WESTMINSTER, THE HOUSE OF LORDS: royal entrance, royal gallery, library and committee rooms, 1822–7; partly destroyed by fire 1834, remainder demolished 1851.

LONDON, ST. PETER'S CHURCH, WALWORTH, 1823–4.

LONDON, THE INSOLVENT DEBTORS' COURT, PORTUGAL STREET, LINCOLN'S INN FIELDS, 1823–4; demolished 1911.

LONDON, BOARD OF TRADE AND PRIVY COUNCIL OFFICES, WHITEHALL, 1824–6; remodelled by Barry 1845–6.

WESTMINSTER, THE HOUSE OF COMMONS: LIBRARY and COMMITTEE ROOMS, 1826–7, Gothic; destroyed by fire 1834.

LONDON, HOLY TRINITY CHURCH, MARYLEBONE, 1826–7; chancel 1878; converted into S.P.C.K. offices 1955–6.

LONDON, ST. JOHN'S CHURCH, BETHNAL GREEN, 1826–8; interior remodelled after fire in 1870 and chancel extended 1888.

LONDON, FREEMASONS' HALL, GREAT QUEEN STREET, the new COUNCIL CHAMBER, 1828; demolished 1864.

LONDON, THE BANQUETING HOUSE, WHITEHALL, restoration of exterior, 1829–33.

WESTMINSTER, THE STATE PAPER OFFICE, DUKE STREET, 1830–4; demolished 1862

MISCELLANEOUS WORKS

BURY ST. EDMUNDS, SUFFOLK, NO. 81 GUILDHALL STREET, enlarged for James Oakes, 1789–90.

READING, BERKSHIRE, SIMONDS' BREWERY, new house and brewery buildings on east side of Bridge Street, 1789–91; demolished 1900.

NORWICH, SURREY STREET, additions to house (now Norwich Union Fire Office) for John Patterson, 1790.

WINCHESTER, HAMPSHIRE, school (now drill-hall) for the Rev. Mr. Richards, 1795.

MONUMENTS

KENSINGTON, ST. MARY ABBOTS CHURCHYARD, monument to Miss Elizabeth Johnstone for the earl of Bellamont, 1784.

FELBRIDGE PLACE, SURREY, column in memory of James Evelyn, 1785–6, moved to Lemington, Northumberland, 1928.

LONDON, ST. STEPHEN'S CHURCH, COLEMAN STREET, monument to Claude Bosanquet, 1786; destroyed by bombing 1940.

LEYTONSTONE CHURCHYARD, ESSEX, monument to Samuel Bosanquet, 1806; demolished 1957–8.

SOUTHWARK CATHEDRAL, tablet in south choir aisle to Abraham Newland, 1808.

CHISWICK CHURCHYARD, MIDDLESEX, monument to P. J. de Loutherbourg, R.A., 1812.

CRICKET ST. THOMAS CHURCH, SOMERSET, monument to the 1st Viscount Bridport, 1814.

ST. GILES' BURIAL GROUND (now St. Pancras Gardens), monument to Mrs. Soane, 1816.

LAMBETH PARISH CHURCH, monument to Anna Storace, 1817; destroyed.

SIR JOHN SOANE'S MUSEUM, 13 Lincoln's Inn Fields, WC2, is open from Tuesday to Saturday each week, 10am to 5pm. Closed on Sunday, Monday and Bank Holidays. Lecture tour every Saturday, 2.30pm. Enquiries to the Curator at the Museum.

Selected Bibliography

Published works by Soane:

Designs in Architecture, consisting of Plans, Elevations and Sections for Temples, Baths, Casinos, Pavilions, Garden-Seats, Obelisks, and Other Buildings, 1778

Plans, Elevations and Sections of Buildings erected in the Counties of Norfolk, Suffolk, etc., 1788

Sketches in Architecture, containing Plans and Elevations of Cottages, Villas and Other Useful Buildings, 1793

Designs for Public Improvements, 1827 reprinted with additions as *Designs for Public and Private Buildings*, 1828

Description of the House and Museum, etc., 1832 (privately printed), enlarged 1835–36

Memoirs of the Professional Life of an Architect, 1835 (privately printed)

Works on Soane:

Bolton, A. T., ed. *The Works of Sir John Soane, R. A.*, 1924

——, ed. *The Portrait of Sir John Soane, R. A.*, 1927

——, ed. *Lectures on Architecture*, 1929

Birnstingl, H. J., *Sir John Soane*, 1925

Britton, J., *A brief memoir of Sir John Soane*, 1834

Donaldson, T. L., *Review of the Professional Life of Sir John Soane*, 1837

Du Prey, P. de la R., *John Soane, the making of an architect*, 1982

Steele, H. R. and F. R. Yerbury, *The Old Bank of England*, 1930

Summerson, John, *Sir John Soane*, 1952

A New Description of Sir John Soane's Museum, 1955, 4th revised edition 1977 (published by the Trustees)

Stroud, Dorothy, *The Architecture of Sir John Soane*, 1961

——, *Sir John Soane, Architect*, 1983

Articles:

Bolton, A. T., 'Sir John Soane, R.A., F.R.S. F.S.A., 1753–1837', *R.I.B.A. Journal*, 44, 1937, pp. 273–75

Kirklington, J., 'The Soanian Sonnet', *Interiors*, April 1982, pp. 80–99, with photographs of Soane's house by Richard Bryant

Summerson, John, 'Le Tombeau de Sir John Soane', *Revue de l'Art*, No. 30, 1975

——, 'Sir John Soane and the Furniture of Death', *Architectural Review*, March 1978

——, 'At Sir John Soane's Museum', Pidgeon Audio Visual, PAV 792, with photographs by John Donat

Teyssot, G., 'John Soane and the Birth of Style', *Oppositions*, 14, 1978, pp. 67–75, also published in French as 'John Soane et la naissance du style', *Archives d'Architecture Moderne*, No. 21, 1981, pp. 25–46

On Dulwich Picture Gallery
Primary Sources:

Binney, M., 'London's First Picture Gallery', *Country Life*, 147, 1970, pp. 230–34

Blanch, W. H., *Ye Parish of Camberwell: Its History and Antiquities*, 1875

Britton, J., *A Brief Catalogue of Pictures, late the property of Sir Francis Bourgeois, R.A.*, 1813

Cockburn, R., *A Catalogue of the Dulwich Gallery*, 1816

Cook, E., *Catalogue of the Pictures in the Gallery of Alleyn's College of God's Gift at Dulwich*, 1914

Desenfans, N. J., *A Descriptive Catalogue of some Pictures of the Different Schools purchased for His Majesty the late King of Poland*, 1802

——, *Memoirs of the late Noel Desenfans Esq. containing also a plan for preserving the portraits of Distinguished Characters etc.*, 1810

Elmes, J., *Annals of the Fine arts*, 1818

Gordon Roe, F., 'London's Forgotten Gallery', *The Connoisseur*, 90, 1932, pp. 257–62

Manning, O., and W. Bray, *The History and Topography of the County of Surrey*, Vol. 25, 1847, pp. 433–50

Patmore, P. G., *Beauties of the Dulwich Picture Gallery*, 1824

Richter, J. P., and J. C. L. Sparkes, *A Descriptive and Historical Catalogue with Biographical Notices of the Painters*, 1880

Rykwert, J., 'The Architecture of Dulwich Picture Gallery', *The Listener*, 71, No. 1, 1964, pp. 158–59

Smith, J. T., *Nollekens and his Times*, 1828, Vol. I

Sparkes, J. C. L., *A Descriptive Catalogue with Biographical Notices of the Painters*, 1876

Summerly, F., (alias H. Cole), *A Handbook for the Dulwich Picture Gallery*, 1842

Warner, G., *Catalogue of Manuscripts and Monuments in Dulwich College*, 1881

Young, W., *The History of Dulwich College*, Vol. I., 1889

Secondary Sources:

Banwell, D. G., ed. *Alleyn's College of God's Gift 350th Anniversary, 1619–1969. A Catalogue of pictures, documents and photographs illustrating the history of the Foundation, 1969*

——, ed. *Alleyn's College of God's Gift 350th Anniversary 1619–1969 Magazine*, 1969

Cornforth, J., 'Displaying Concern for Paintings', *Country Life*, 169, 1981, pp. 1592–96

Gray, G., 'The Pictures at Dulwich', *In Britain*, November 1971

Hall, E. T., *Dulwich History and Romance AD 967–1916*, 1917

Kelly, G., 'Dulwich Picture Gallery', *Museums Journal*, 55, 1955, pp. 10–12

Oswald, A., 'Edward Alleyn's College of God's Gift', *Country Life*, 132, 1962, pp. 1272–74

ACKNOWLEDGEMENTS

Our thanks go to Sir John Summerson, Curator, and to Miss Christine Scull, Library Assistant, of the Sir John Soane Museum for their considerable help in the preparation of this monograph; to Howard Colvin and John Murray, Publishers; to the National Monuments Record; and to all those who have in some way contributed to this publication.

PHOTOGRAPHIC CREDITS

Our thanks go to the following contributors of illustrative material: Bibliothèque Nationale, Paris p42 bottom; *Connaissance des Arts* p21; *Country Life* p47 14, p50 22; National Monuments Record: p44 9, p47 15, p48 17, p66 7, p94 44, p106 top left, p107 top right, p111 top; p74 26 (*Arch. & Bldg News*); p113 top right (G. Barnes); p74 24, p75 27 (Batsford); p43 7 (S. Blutman); p55 32 (A. Colebrook); p43 6, p103 top, p106 bottom, interiors, p110 bottom right (H. Felton); p107 bottom right (H. Gernsheim); p106 top right (B. Lemere); p107 top right (G. Mason); p113 top right (S. W. Newbury); p55 31 (Norfolk Photo. Ill.); p111 bottom right (A. J. Pound); p52 25–26 (Mrs Tomlinson); p44 8, p57 37, p66 6, p67 8–11, p70 16, p71 17–19, p74 23, 25, p110 top right (F. R. Yerbury); Soane Museum: front and back covers, flaps, p2, p3, p6, p10 2, p11 4, p12 5–6, p13 7, p15 8–10, p16 11, p17 12–13, p18 14, p19 15, p20 16, p22 18, p23 19, p25 2–3, p26 4–6, p27 7–8, p28 9–11, p29 12–14, p30 15, p31 16–18, p34 23–24, p36 26–27, p37 28–31, p38 32, p39 33–34, p42 4, p45 10–11, p46 13, p59 39, p60 1, p61 2, p62 3, p63 4, pp64–65 5, p68 12–13, p69 14–15, p72 20–21, p73 22, p76 1, p77 2, p78 3–6, p79 7–8, p80 9–10, p81 11–13, p82 14, 16, p84 20–21, p85 22–24, p86 26, 28, p87 29, p88 30, p89 32–33, p90 35, p92 37–39, p93 42–43, p95 45, p96 46, p97 47, p100, p101, p104, p105, p106 bottom left, p107 bottom left, p108, p109, p110 top and bottom left, p111 bottom left and centre, p112; p8, p24, p32, p33 (Margaret Harker); Victoria and Albert Museum: p84 25, p86 27. The following illustrations are from Soane publications: p45 11, p111 bottom left (*Professional Life*); p46 13, p107 bottom left, p111 bottom centre (*Public and Private Buildings*). Colour photography of paintings and drawings in the Soane Museum is by Richard Cheatle, except p34 24, p38 32, p39 33–34, pp64–65 5, p69 15, p76 1 and gatefolds V and VI which are by Dennis Crompton. Colour photograph on p35 is copyright Academy Editions.

Résumé en français

Dans son essai littéraire 'Soane: L'homme et le Style', version revue et corrigée de son livre *Sir John Soame* (1952), Sir John Summerson identifie les éléments caractéristiques du style Soane tout d'abord avec une vue d'ensemble sur la carrière de l'architecte, pour ensuite étudier sa vie professionnelle pendant les années formatrices. Le style Soane est une des curiosités de l'architecture européenne et, lorsqu'il atteint sa plénitude dans les années 1790, aucun architecte n'était, en Europe, aussi dégagé des contraintes de loyauté envers le classicisme, aussi libre dans sa manipulation des proportions et aussi aventureux en structure et en éclairage que ne l'était Soane pour la Bank of England à l'époque.

La carrière de Soane se divise en cinq périodes: la période d'études, 1776–80 (de 23 à 27 ans), principalement influencée par le néo-classicisme français; la période de début de carrière, 1780–91 (de 27 à 38 ans), pendant laquelle il construisit des petites maisons de campagne influencées par Wyatt et Holland; la période intermédiaire, 1791–1806 (de 38 à 53 ans), période la plus créatrice pendant laquelle il obtint de nombreux postes et où les différents éléments formant le style Soane prirent naissance; la période Pittoresque, 1806–21 (de 53 à 68 ans), période tourmentée de sa vie privée qui vit les éléments de son style se remanier pour obtenir des effets Pittoresques nouveaux qu'il appela 'la Poésie de l'Architecture'; la période finale, 1821–33 (de 68 à 80 ans), une période solitaire où il conçut des bâtiments publics mal accueillis par les critiques et qui marqua un retour au néo-classicisme.

Summerson attire l'attention sur un nombre de thèmes appartenant à la période créatrice intermédiaire et démontre comment Soane les développa et les déploya dans la période Pittoresque. Ces thèmes comprennent le dôme en pendentif et l'oculus, les fenêtres semi-circulaires sur les arches à segments, le toit en contreclef, et la substitution de l'ordre classique par des rangées de pilastres, symptôme du 'primitivisme' de Laugier que Soane adopta. Ce style si caractéristique se développa rapidement et totalement entre l'âge de 38 et 45 ans; avant cela son travail fut soit dérivatif soit sans succès. Pendant la période Pittoresque, ainsi dénommée à cause de son analogie aux oeuvres des paysagistes et théoriciens de l'école Pittoresque, les thèmes existants furent remaniés et réinterprétés sans qu'il n'en fut ajouté de nouveaux. Ce fut aussi pendant cette période que Soane vint à voir son propre style comme unissant les potentialités tout aussi

bien des différents types de classicisme que de gothique.

Ce que doit Soane à George Dance, avec lequel il étudia dans son jeune âge, est indéniable; preuve en est même faite, dans certains cas, par des esquisses de Dance comprenant des études préliminaires pour la Bank Stock Office. Il ne s'agit pas, bien sûr, de suggérer que le travail de Soane est celui de Dance sous clef, la griffe de Soane étant si différente et si personnalisée; ce qui est indéniable est que le style Soane ne découle pas des efforts d'un seul homme mais de deux, et Soane ne manqua jamais d'exprimer sa reconnaissance.

Summerson termine par le récit des dernières années de Soane lorsqu'il cessa ses activités, à l'âge de 80 ans, en 1833. A la même époque Soane obtint un Décret du Parlement par lequel, à sa mort, sa maison et son contenu devenaient patrimoine national. Cette légation marquait la fin de son rêve: celui qu'un fils architecte lui succède, rêve qu'il poursuivit avec tant de ténacité qu'il conduisit ses fils à la rébellion. La collection du Museum ne cessa de s'agrandir jusqu'à sa mort en 1837, avec la remarquable acquisition des peintures *Election* par Hogarth et le Sarcophage de Belzoni; le Museum tient aujourd'hui place de monument à la mémoire de Soane, révérant la profession qu'il aima avec tant de passion.

L'essai de David Watkin 'Soane et ses Contemporains', traite des similarités—et des différences—dans le travail de Soane et ses contemporains tant dans son pays qu'à l'étranger. Soane nous présente le paradoxe d'un défenseur dévoué à la tradition classique en architecture et d'un artiste romantique suivant un chemin solitaire dans un style idiosyncratique, son travail devant son piquant visuel et intellectuel à la tension fructueuse entre la doctrine publique et l'expérience personnelle. Etudier Soane c'est se trouver face au problème de l'expression de la personnalité dans l'architecture, son travail reflétant les qualités fondamentales de son caractère.

Ainsi que de nombreux architectes anglais, Soane fit un voyage d'études en Italie, une expérience qui ne s'arrêta pas à l'étude d'une série déterminée de monuments, mais qui lui permit de se familiariser avec l'approche des gagnants des Grand Prix français. Comme tous les architectes avant-garde de cette époque, Soane produisit un certain nombre de projets chimériques néo-classiques mais, contrairement aux autres, ces projets le préoccupèrent constamment par la

suite; ce fut ainsi pour le Pont Triomphal (un Grand Prix français standard) vers lequel il est continuellement retourné au fil des années. Soane doit énormément aux romantiques de la tradition classique française, en particulier à Le Camus de Mezières et E.L. Boullée. Le désir d'acquérir un style si personnel qu'il le différencierait totalement de ses contemporains semble découler en partie de sa familiarité avec la théorie française, illustré aussi par l'intérêt qu'il portait à la structure gothique pure des cathédrales et autres bâtiments publics.

L'influence profonde de Laugier, dont les doctrines réductionnistes ont animé les excellents essais littéraires palladiens sélectionnés pour être publiés dans *Plans, Elevations and Sections etc.*, de 1788, apparaît aussi dans les cours qu'il donna à la Royal Academy à partir de 1809. Non seulement il condamne les éléments anti-fonctionnels, conformément aux principes anti-ornementaux de Laugier, et par cela censurant certaines de ses intentions les plus précieuses, mais il se dissocie des doctrines de Chambers dont le *Treatise* considérait les ordres comme étant principalement décoratifs.

Mis à part le travail de George Dance, il est évident que d'autres architectes suivaient la même voie que Soane et ceci est illustré par le travail de Thomas Leverton, John Tasker et S.P. Cockerell en Angleterre, et Benjamin Latrobe aux Etats-Unis, surtout dans les intérieurs créés pour le Capitol à Washington D.C.. Le célèbre contemporain de Soane, John Nash, n'est que superficiellement proche de Soane en tant que protagoniste du Pittoresque et diffère si évidemment dans les principes fondamentaux. Nash opta pour un système d'éclairage directe, comme celui de Soane, dans les galeries de sa maison et à Buckingham Palace.

La façon dont Soane dissout les formes architecturales en espaces évidés et poétiquement éclairés est similaire aux oeuvres antérieures du peintre J.M.W. Turner, ami de Soane, une de leurs préoccupations principales à tous deux étant la lumière. La représentation picturale de l'architecture par la voie d'attrayantes aquarelles dont Turner fut un précurseur, fut un produit naturel de la sensibilité Pittoresque, et les plaques figurant dans *Sketches in Architecture* de Soane (1793), ainsi que les grandes aquarelles que produisit son atelier à l'époque, sont très proches du travail de Turner. Soane travailla avec Turner à la préparation de dessins d'étude lorsque celui-ci fut Professeur de Perspective à la Royal Academy, et il apparaît clairement, au travers des modifications de Soane, que l'intérêt que Turner portait à la représentation de la lumière en peinture n'était pas moins important que leur soucis de mettre en valeur les tableaux exposés. L'influence de Soane sur Turner est évidente dans la maison italianisée et la galerie de peinture qu'il se fit construire en 1819–21.

Il est possible de trouver des parallèles aux oeuvres de Soane dans le travail d'architectes anglais tels que John Foulson (1772–1842), James Spiller (c.1760–1829), David Laing (1774–1856), Thomas Harrison (1774–1829), John Dobson (1787–1865), Sir Jeffrey Wyatville (1766–1840) et W.J. Donthorn (1799–1859). Nous trouvons, d'autre part, d'importantes affinités avec le travail de Soane et le style franco-prussien des années 1800, dans le travail d'architectes tels que les deux Gilly, Gentz et Weinbrenner. Schinkel, bien que de la génération suivante, a des similarités dans la ligne que prit sa carrière et dans sa manière de traiter les formes architecturales afin de produire des effets linéaires et contreignants, Pittoresques et poétiques.

En conclusion, Watkin cite, parmi les nombreux exemples de source contemporaine, quelques-unes des critiques auxquelles Soane fut assujetti dans sa carrière, faisant ainsi ressortir son isolement au milieu de ses contemporains, avec lesquels il avait si peu d'affinités.

Dans son article intitulé 'Dulwich Picture Gallery *Revisited*', G.-Tilman Mellinghoff nous résume l'histoire de la galerie et nous éclaire sur la complexité des différents stades de conception de ce monument que Soane créa pour son ami Sir P. Francis Bourgeois qui légua quelques 360 tableaux. La galerie de Dulwich fut conçue par Soane en 1811, époque de plénitude pendant laquelle il atteignit son propre style introspectif. Ce monument est considéré par beaucoup comme chef-d'oeuvre et fut un travail très cher à Soane, auquel il voua d'intenses efforts, comme on peut en juger ne serait-ce que par la quantité, la diversité et l'inconsistence des maquettes qui existent encore.

L'intention première de Bourgeois était l'érection d'un mausolée en marbre comme celui que Soane fit construire pour son ami Noel Desenfans, qui fut à l'origine de cette collection, et dont les tableaux devaient être déposés dans la galerie de l'ancien Collège, adaptée et remise en état. Soane eut, dès le début, clairement l'intention de reconstruire, et les cinq premiers projets qu'il soumit en mai 1811 furent pour un nouveau collège en quadrangle, ne conservant de l'ancien collège que la chapelle. Bien que ces projets furent rejetés pendant les guerres napoléoniennes, Soane fut, typiquement, fidèle à cette idée et les projets suivants comprenaient tous la galerie dans un collège en quadrangle.

La galerie émergea progressivement de cette idée de quadrangle. Dans les premiers projets, deux différentes versions de stylistiques apparaissent qui, toutes deux, tendent vers une insertion harmonieuse avec la chapelle, tout en créant une tension entre les éléments classiques et gothiques, mais aucune n'y réussit vraiment. Il s'ensuivit une série de tentatives dans lesquelles les plans furent réorganisés, les derniers montrant des projets beaucoup plus sobres et demandant un remaniement substantiel de stylistique et qui formèrent le troisième stade, et le dernier, du projet. La recherche d'une solution moins coûteuse pourvut une version plus simple et dépouillée et dont le remaniement extrêmement simplifié des thèmes classiques reste frappant. Même après que la première pierre fut posée en octobre 1811, il y eut un changement majeur: le mausolée fut transposé de la face est à la face ouest, créant ainsi une impression différente. La construction fut très rapide; la galerie elle-même fut terminée dans le courant de 1813, les tableaux arrivèrent en 1814 et la galerie fut ouverte en 1815.

Bien qu'il soit tentant d'apparenter la Galerie de Dulwich aux projets de musées pour les Grands Prix français, il semble qu'il y ait plus de points communs avec la tradition anglaise de galeries privées de résidences provinciales dont l'évolution architecturale débute avec la fin de la traditionnelle galerie en longueur. Dans son projet, en 1787, pour une galerie à Fonthill House, Soane opta pour une division de la galerie traditionnelle en longueur, alors qu'à Dulwich le changement intervient par la transition de galerie privée en galerie publique. Un certain nombre de galeries importantes fut construit juste avant Dulwich, dont la Galerie à Castle Howard par C.H. Tatham (1801–12) se rapprocha le plus mais, à l'encontre de celles-ci, Dulwich fut la première galerie à donner une expression externe à la fonction interne et, dans ce sens, est unique en son genre.

Le mausolée fut ce que considéra Soane comme la partie la plus importante de Dulwich, un microcosme de l'ensemble et une réalisation sublime de l'idée Romantique de la mort transcendantale. Son intégration dans l'ensemble fut une idée de Soane et, comme pour Gilly, probablement inspirée de la coutume médiévale où la tombe du fondateur était placée dans l'église. Le mausolée donne l'impression d'une décoration grèque subtile avec une atmosphère byzantine, une lanterne dissimulée projetant une douce lumière ambrée dans la salle du sarcophage, créant ainsi la 'lumière mystérieuse' que Soane admirait dans les églises françaises.

Le système d'éclairage par le haut n'était utilisé à l'époque que dans les expositions londoniennes et dans les salles de vente où l'on avait tant besoin de l'espace mural, mais après l'impact que produisit la galerie de Fonthill de Soane, cela devint le moyen à la mode, comme en témoignent les galeries de Petworth, Panshanger, Brocklesby et Attingham. Ce système d'éclairage, et l'architecture elle-même, furent sujets à de fortes critiques à l'époque et plus tard. De part sa contestation de la validité des règles classiques, le projet de Dulwich ne pouvait qu'irriter et dérouter ses contemporains.

Une série d'annexes aux 19e et 20e siècles transformèrent ce bâtiment qui passa de cinq pièces en suite à une triple rangée de quatorze pièces.

En conclusion, Dulwich ne fut pas un projet ordinaire pour Soane; ce fut son projet le plus attachant, non seulement bénévole mais qu'il était prêt à financer lui-même quant il rencontra des difficultés financières. Ce projet, au milieu de ce cadre rural idéal, fut une sorte de défi par lequel il vit son amitié avec Bourgeois s'épanouir. Résultant d'un travail laborieux et assidu, et conçu en plusieurs étapes, Dulwich naquit d'un projet assez modeste à l'origine pour devenir l'une des expressions les plus individuelles de Soane en architecture, et considéré par beaucoup comme le summum de sa réussite.

Deutsche Zusammenfassung

Sir John Summerson bestimmt in seinem Essay 'Soane: The Man and the Style', einer überarbeiteten Fassung seines Buches *Sir John Soane* (1952), die charakteristischen Elemente des Stils von Soane. Er zeichnet zunächst ein allgemeines Bild von dem Werdegang des Architekten und geht dann auf dessen berufliche Entwicklung in den entscheidenden Jahren seines Lebens ein. Soanes Stil, in den 90er Jahren des 18. Jahrhunderts zur Reife gelangt, zählt zu den Kuriositäten der europäischen Architektur. Es gab zu jener Zeit keinen anderen Architekten in Europa, der so ungezwungen mit der Loyalität zur Klassik umging, so frei in der Handhabung von Proportionen und so kühn in Bezug auf Struktur und Beleuchtung war wie Soane bei der Bank von England.

Soanes Werdegang vollzieht sich in fünf Zeitabschnitten: die Studienzeit 1776–80 (Alter 23–27), die hauptsächlich beeinflußt war vom französischen Klassizismus; die Zeit der ersten praktischen Tätigkeit 1780–91 (Alter 27–38), in der sich Soane, beeinflußt von Wyatt und Holland, hauptsächlich mit dem Bau kleinerer Landhäuser beschäftigte; die mittlere Periode 1791–1806 (Alter 38–53), die kreativste Phase in Soanes Karriere, seine Tätigkeit für verschiedene Büros, eine Zeit, in der die charakteristischen Elemente seines Stils zum Durchbruch kamen; die pittoreske Phase 1806–21 (Alter 53–68), geprägt von den Schwierigkeiten in Soanes Privatleben, in der er seine Stilelemente neu zusammenstellte, um besondere pittoreske Effekte zu erzielen, was von ihm 'Poetry of Architecture' genannt wurde; und der letzte Abschnitt seiner Karriere 1821–33 (Alter 68–80), den Soane in Einsamkeit und heftiger Kritik ausgesetzt mit dem Entwerfen großer öffentlicher Gebäude verbrachte, eine Zeit, in der er zum Klassizismus zurückkehrte.

Summerson macht auf eine Anzahl verschiedener Themen aufmerksam, die in Soanes schöpferische mittlere Periode fallen und zeigt, wie er diese in der späteren pittoresken Phase entwickelt oder erweitert hat. Es geht um die schwebende Kuppel mit dem Okulus, die Halbrundfenster über den Segmentbögen, das Vierungsgewölbe und die Substitution einer klassischen Säulenordnung durch Lisene, ein Zeichen dafür, daß Soane Laugiers 'Primitivism' anerkannt hat. Soanes charakteristischer Stil bildete sich schnell und vollständig aus als er im Alter von 30–45 Jahren war. Vor dieser Zeit waren seine Projekte entweder Derivate oder nicht erfolgreich. Während seiner pittoresken Phase, so genannt weil sein Werk dem der Landschaftsmaler und Theoretiker

der pittoresken Schule ähnlich war, wurden die vorhandenen Themen neu geordnet und interpretiert, ohne daß neue hinzukamen. In dieser Zeit betrachtete Soane seinen Stil auch als eine Vereinigung nicht nur verschiedener Arten des Klassizismus, sondern auch der Gothik.

Es gibt keinen Zweifel daran, daß Soane seinem Lehrer George Dance viel zu verdanken hat. In einigen Fällen liefern Skizzen von Dance den Dokumentarischen Beweis dafür, vor allem seine vorläufigen Skizzen für das Bank Stock Office. Das heißt nicht, daß irgendeins von Soanes architektonischen Werken Dance 'sous clef' ist, denn sie unterscheiden sich beträchtlich von Dance und haben das unverwechselbare Soanesche Temperament. Soanes Stil ist dennoch ohne Zweifel nicht nur das Werk eines Mannes, sondern das von zweien, was Soane niemals verhehlt hat.

Summerson beschließt sein Essay mit einem Abriß über die letzten Jahre in Soanes Leben, nachdem er 1833 im Alter von 80 Jahren in den Ruhestand getreten war. Im Jahre 1833 erlangte er das persönliche Parlamentsgesetz, das besagte, daß sein Haus mitsamt Inhalt eine nationale Institution nach seinem Tod werden würde. Diese Entscheidung, seinen Besitz aufzugeben, markierte das Ende seines Traumes, daß seine Architektensöhne sein Amt einmal übernehmen würden, ein dynastisches Ideal, für das er so ernsthaft gekämpft hat, daß es seine Söhne zur Revolte gegen ihn trieb. Das Museum vergrößerte sich noch bis zu seinem Tod im Jahre 1837 durch den bemerkenswerten Erwerb der Hogarth 'Election'-Gemälde und des Belzoni-Sarkophags. Heute steht es als Denkmal im Dienste jenes Berufsstandes, den er mit solch wilder Leidenschaft geliebt hat.

David Watkins Essay 'Soane and his Contemporaries' behandelt die Ähnlichkeiten und die Unterschiede in Soanes Werk verglichen mit dem seiner Zeitgenossen im In- und Ausland. Soane konfrontiert uns mit dem Widerspruch, einerseits ein engagierter Verteidiger der klassischen Tradition in der Architektur, andererseits ein romantischer Künstler gewesen zu sein, der einen einsamen Weg mit einem eigenwilligen Stil verfolgte, wobei die visuelle und intellektuelle Schärfe seines Werkes von der fruchtbaren Spannung zwischen allgemeingültiger Lehrmeinung und persönlicher Anschauung herrührte. Soane zu studieren heißt, mit dem Problem des Ausdrucks von Persönlichkeit in der Architektur konfrontiert zu sein, denn in seinem Werk spiegeln sich seine

fundamentalen Charaktereigenschaften wieder.

Soane hat wie viele Architekten eine Studienreise nach Italien unternommen. Dieses Erlebnis war nicht nur auf das Studium klassischer Monumente beschränkt, sondern beinhaltete auch das Kennenlernen der architektonischen Einstellungen französischer Grand-Prix-Gewinner. Wie die meisten stilistisch fortgeschrittenen Architekten jener Zeit hat Soane eine Anzahl visionärer neoklassizistischer Projekte entworfen. Aber dadurch, daß er sich fortgesetzt mit ihnen beschäftigte wie im Falle des Entwurfs einer triumphalen Brücke (ein Standard Grand-Prix-Projekt), zu dem er über Jahre hinweg immer wieder zurückkehrte, unterschied er sich von ihnen. Soane hat den Romantikern innerhalb der französischen klassischen Tradition viel zu verdanken, vor allen Dingen Le Camus de Mezières and E. L. Boullée. Das Bestreben, eine so persönliche Haltung zu entwickeln, die ihn von seinen Zeitgenossen abhob, scheint teilweise von der Kenntnis französischer Theorie zu kommen, teilweise von seinem Interesse an der Struktur gothischer Kathedralen und anderer öffentlicher Gebäude aus dieser Zeit. Der tiefgehende Einfluß von Laugier, dessen reduktionistischen Grundsätze die eleganten Essays über Palladio, die Soane für seine Publikation *Plans, Elevations and Sections* (1788) ausgewählt hatte, beleben, findet sich wieder in seinen Vorlesungen, die er ab 1809 in der Royal Academy gehalten hat. Er verurteilte nicht nur anti-funktionale Elemente in Übereinstimmung mit Laugiers anti-ornamentalen Prinzipien, womit er einige seiner besten Interieure zensierte, sondern distanzierte sich auch von den Grundsätzen Chambers, dessen *Treatise* die klassischen Ordnungen als hauptsächlich dekorativ ansieht.

Außer im Werk von George Dance finden sich Anzeichen, daß andere Architekten eine ähnliche Linie wie Soane verfolgt haben im Werk von Thomas Leverton, John Tasker und S. P. Cockerell in England und Benjamin Latrobe in Amerika, besonders in seinem Soane-ähnlichen Interieur für das Capitol in Washington. Soanes berühmter Zeitgenosse John Nash steht ihm oberflächlich gesehen nahe als ein Exponent des Pittoresken, unterscheidet sich aber wesentlich in allen Grundlagen. Nash verwandte in den Galerien für sein eigenes Haus und Buckingham Palast ein System der Beleuchtung von oben, das dem Soanes ähnlich war.

Soanes Auflösung von architektonischen Formen in poetisch beleuchtete Hohlräume ist ebenfalls vergleichbar mit dem Spätwerk des Malers und persönlichen Freundes J. M. W. Turner, denn für beide war 'Licht' das zentrale Thema. Architektur in reizvollen Aquarellen darzustellen, worin Turner ein Pionier war, war die natürliche Folge der Sensibilität für das Pittoreske. Die Tafeln in Soanes *Sketches in Architecture* (1793) und die großen Aquarelle, die in seinem Büro hergestellt wurden, stehen dem Werk Turners sehr nahe. Soane hat mit Turner bei der Vorbereitung von Demonstrations-Zeichnungen zusammengearbeitet, als Turner Professor für Perspektive an der Royal Academy war. Von den Veränderungen, die er dort einführte, ist ersichtlich, daß Turners Beschäftigung mit Licht in der Malerei begleitet war von dem Bemühen um eine angemessene Technik der Bilder, was er mit Soane gemeinsam hatte. Soanes Einfluß auf Turner manifestiert sich in einem Entwurf für ein Haus im italienischen Stil mit Gemäldegalerie, das in den Jahren 1819–21 gebaut wurde.

Parallelen zu dem Werk von Soane finden sich in den Werken der englischen Architekten John Foulson (1772–1842), James Spiller (c. 1760–1829), David Laing (1774–1856), Thomas Harrison (1774–1829), John Dobson (1787–1865), Sir Jeffrey Wyatville (1766–1840) und W. J. Donthorn (1799–1859). Im Ausland zeigen sich große Ähnlichkeiten zwischen Soane und dem Franco-Preußischen Stil von der Zeit um 1800, im Werk von Architekt i c̈lteren und jüngeren Gilly, Gentz und Weinbrenner. Schinkel, obwohl eine generation jünger als Soane, ist ihm verwandt in dem Sinne, daß seine Laufbahn ähnlich verlief und auch in der Art und Weise wie er architektonische Formen handhabe um Effekte zu erzielen, die linear und streng oder pittoresk und poetisch waren. Zum Schluß zitiert Watkin aus einer Anzahl zeitgenössischer Quellen einige der Kritiken, denen der Architekt während seines Lebens ausgesetzt war und unterstreicht Soanes isolation von seinen Zeitgenossen, mit denen er so wenig gemeinsam hatte.

G.- Tilman Mellinghoff gibt in seinem Artikel 'Dulwich Picture Gallery *Revisited*' ein zusammengefaßtes Bild von der Geschichte des Gebäudes und erläutert den komplexen Entwurfsprozeß, mit dem Soane ein einmaliges Monument für seinen engen Freund Sir P. Francis Bourgeois und seinem Vermächtnis von 360 Bildern an das College geschaffen hat. Dulwich Picture Gallery wurde von Soane im Jahre 1811 entworfen als er auf dem Höhepunkt seines Lebens war und zu seinem eigenen, innerlichen Stil gelangt war. Von vielen wurde dieses Werk als Soanes größte Errungenschaft betrachtet. Es war ihm besonders lieb und er widmete ihm viel persönliche Energie, was sich in der Menge,

Unterschiedlichkeit und Unvereinbarkeit der erhalten gebliebenen Pläne ausdrückt.

Bourgeois ursprünglicher Auftrag war die Errichtung eines Marmor Mausoleums, das dem nachgebildet sein sollte, welches Soane ihm für seinen Freund Noel Desenfans, dem Initiator der Sammlung gebaut hatte. Die Bilder sollten in der alten College-Galerie untergebracht werden, nachdem diese entsprechend hergerichtet und restauriert worden war. Aber Soane beabsichtigte von Anfang an, neu zu bauen. Die ersten fünf Entwürfe, die er im Mai 1811 vorlegte, sahen einen rechteckigen College-komplex vor, in dem nur die alte Kapelle beibehalten war. Obwohl sie für die Zeit der Napoleonischen Krieg zurückgestellt wurden, ließ Soane die Idee niemals fallen, was typisch für ihn war; und in allen darauffolgenden Entwürfen wird die Galerie also Teil eines neu zu bauenden rechteckigen College-Komplexes konzipiert.

Die Galerie entwickelte sich also allmählich aus der Idee des rechteckigen Gebäudekomplexes. In den ersten Entwürfen gibt es zwei verschiedene stilistische Versionen, beide ein Ausdruck des Bestrebens, ein harmonisches Ensemble mit der vorhandenen Kapelle zu schaffen, beide ein Ausdruck der Spannung zwischen klassischen und gothischen Elementen, aber keine von beiden wirklich gelungen. Danach folgte eine Reihe von Versuchen, die Pläne neu zu organisieren. Im dritten und letzten Stadium zeigten sie ein viel schlichteres Design und verlangten nach einer substantiellen stilistischen Umgestaltung des Entwurfs. Die Suche nach einer weniger kostspieligen Lösung öffnete den Weg zu einer sehr schlichten Version, bei der die drastisch simplifizierte Neuformulierung von klassischen Themen auffallend ist. Sogar noch nach der Grundsteinlegung im Oktober 1811 gab es eine größere Veränderung. Das Mausoleum wurde von der Ost- zur Westfassade gebracht, wodurch eine andere Betonung erreicht wurde. Der Bau machte schnelle Fortschritte; der Rohbau für die Galerie war Mitte 1813 fertig, die Bilder trafen im Jahre 1814 ein und die Eröffnung fand im Jahre 1815 statt.

Obwohl es sich anbietet, die Dulwich-Galerie mit den französischen Grand-Prix-Entwürfen für Museen in Zusammenhang zu bringen, ist sie eher der englischen Tradition privater Landhaus-Galerien verwandt, bei denen die architektonische Weiterentwicklung mit der Aufteilung der traditionellen langen Galerie begann. In seinem Entwurf von 1787 für eine Galerie in Fonthill House fand es Soane notwendig, den Typ der langen Galerie aufzuteilen, aber bei Dulwich geschieht die höchst wichtige Veränderung in ein funktionales Arrangement von

Ausstellungsräumen mit dem Übergang von privater zu öffentlicher Besichtigung. Eine Anzahl wichtiger Galerien war kurz vor Dulwich erbaut worden, von denen ihr die Castle-Howard-Galerie von C. H. Tatham (1801–12) am nächsten kam. Aber im Unterschied zu diesen Vorläufern war Dulwich die erste, bei der die inneren Funktionen ihren Ausdruck im Äußeren fanden, und somit ist sie einmalig.

Das Mausoleum wurde von Soane als der wichtigste Teil von Dulwich angesehen, als ein Mikrokosmos des Ganzen und als erhabene Realisation der romantizistischen Idee vom transzendenten Tod. Die Kombination mit der Galerie war Soanes eigene Idee und mag—wie im Fall von Gilly—von dem mittelalterlichen Brauch inspiriert worden sein, die Gräber der Gründer in den Kirchen zu haben. Die Wirkung des Mausoleums beruht auf subtiler griechischer Dekoration und byzantinischer Atmosphäre, eine verborgene Laterne bringt gedämpftes Licht in den Raum mit dem Sarkophag um ein 'lumière mystérieuse' zu erzeugen, das Soane so sehr in französischen Kirchen bewundert hat.

Das System der Beleuchtung von oben wurde zu jener Zeit nur in Londoner Ausstellungs- und Auktionsräumen verwandt wegen des großen Bedarfs an Wandflächen, aber Soanes Fonthill-Galerie machte es fast obligatorisch, was durch die Galerien von Petworth, Panshanger, Brocklesby und Attingham bestätigt wird. Die Beleuchtungsart wie die Architektur an sich wurden heftig kritisiert sowohl zu jener Zeit wie auch später. In dem Maße wie die Gültigkeit klassischer Normen in Frage gestellt wurde, war es fast zu erwarten, daß Dulwich seine Zeitgenossen erzürnen und verwirren würde.

Eine Reihe von Erweiterungen des 19. und 20. Jahrhunderts vergrößerten das Gebäude von einer einzelnen Flucht von 5 Räumen zu einer dreifachen von insgesamt 14 Räumen.

Dulwich war kein gewöhnliches Werk von Soane, es war sein persönlichstes, für das er kein Honorar verlangte und bei dem er sogar bereit war, zu bezahlen, wenn finanzielle Schwierigkeiten auftraten. Es war für ihn eine Herausforderung, in der seine Freundschaft mit Bourgeois in einer idealen ländlichen Umgebung ihren Ausdruck fand. Als Resultat eines langsamen und arbeitsintensiven Prozesses mit mehreren Entwurfsstadien, entwickelte sich Dulwich von einem bescheidenen frühen Entwurf zu einer von Soanes höchst individuellen Ausdrucksformen in der Architektur, und wird daher von vielen als der Höhepunkt seiner Errungenschaft betrachtet.

Sommario in Italiano

Nel saggio di Sir John Summerson dal titolo 'Soane l'uome e il suo stile', che é una rielaborazione del suo libro *Sir John Soane* (1952), vengono stabiliti gli elementi fondamentali dello stile Soane, discutendo in un primo luogo il quadro generale della carriera dell'architetto e in un secondo luogo la sua vita professionale durante gli anni formativi. Lo stile Soane é rimasto una delle curiosità dell'architettura europea nel 1790; nessun altro architetto in Europa, in quel periodo, era riuscito a staccarsi dai legami del classicismo come lui o era capace di manipolare le proporzioni o innovare le strutture e l'illuminazione come lui fece allora nella Banca d'Inghilterra.

La carriera di Soane puó essere suddivisa in cinque periodi: Da studente (etá 23–27) dal 1776 al 1780, fu influenzato principalmente dal Neoclassicismo francese; da giovane professionista (etá 27–38) dal 1780 al 1791, construi principalmente piccole residenze di campagna sotto l'influenza dello stile di Wyatt e Holland; il periodo intermedio dal 1791 al 1806 (etá 38–53) é stato il periodo piú creativo della sua carriera, durante il quale ebbe varie ed importanti cariche e dove cominciano ad emergere gli elementi principali dello stile Soane; il periodo pittoresco dal 1806–21 (etá 53–68) comprende un momento difficile nella sua vita personale ed allora gli elementi del suo stile vennero rielaborati per ottenere nuove immagini pittoresche chiamate da lui 'Poesia dell'Architettura'; l'ultimo periodo dal 1821 al 1833 (etá 68–80) fu un periodo triste, di solitudine, durante il quale progettó grandi edifici pubblici, fu criticato e tornó al neoclassicismo.

Summerson elenca vari motivi appartenenti al periodo intermedio di Soane e mostra come vennero ampiati o sviluppati nel successivo periodo pittoresco. Questi motivi sono l'uso della cupola a intraddosso e l'oculus, l'uso di finestre semicircolari sopra ad archi ribassati, l'uso di soffitti a volta a crocera e la sostituzione degli ordini classici con 'pilaster strips' (pilastrini appiattiti), un sintomo del 'primitismo' di Laugier, del quale Soane era un entusiasta. Questo stile di Soane fu sviluppato totalmente e con molta rapidità tra i 38 e 45 anni di etá, prima che le sue opere diventassero imitative o prive di successo. Durante il periodo pittoresco, cosí chiamato perché la sua opera era analoga a quella dei teorici della scuola pittoresca, i motivi esistenti furono riorganizzati o interpretati di nuovo senza che vi venissero aggiunti nuovi temi. E fu anche in questo periodo che Soane inizi^ó a pensare che il suo stile era capace di unificare non solo le possibilità di diversi tipi di classicismo ma anche quelle del Gotico.

Non c'é alcun dubbio sul debito di Soane verso George Dance con cui aveva studiato da giovane; esistono ancora degli schizzi di Dance come evidenza della loro collaborazione, oltre ai primi disegni per l'ufficio borsa della banca. Questo non vuole arrivare a dire che l'opera di Soane é l'opera di Dance 'sous clef', tra l'altro sono molto diverse; quella di Soane ha un temperamento ben preciso. Pero é certo che lo stile di Soane é opera di due persone e Soane lo ammetteva sempre.

Summerson conclude descrivendo gli ultimi anni della vita di Soane dopo il ritiro dalla professione a 80 anni. In quello stesso anno Soane ottenne una dispensa privata dal parlamento per la quale la sua casa ed il suo contenuto sarebbero diventati, dopo la sua morte, museo nazionale. Questa decisione pose fine al sogno di essere succeduto da figli architetti; un ideale al quale era tanto tenacemente attaccato che i suoi figli reagirono ribellandosi ad esso. La collezione del museo continuó ad aumentare fino alla sua morte nel 1837, con l'acquisto delle stampe dell'Elezione di Hogarth e i Sarcofaghi Belzoni. Oggi il museo di Soane rimane il suo personale monumento e allo stesso tempo é utile alla professione, che lui amava con tanta passione.

Il saggio di David Watkin 'Soane e i suoi contemporanei', riguarda le somiglianze—e le differenze—tra l'opera di Soane e quella dei suoi contemporanei, sia in Inghilterra che all'estero—Soane si presenta come il paradosso di un artista che é didicato a conservare la tradizione classica dell'architettura, ma che allo stesso tempo segue la via solitaria del romanticismo con uno stile ideosincratico. La sua opera acquista una intellettuale e visuale vivacitá e freschezza derivata da una fruttifera combinazione di disciplina pubblica e professione privata. Studiare Soane vuol dire affrontare il problema dell'espressione della personalitá nell'architettura, poiché é possibile trovare le principali caratteristiche del suo carattere riflesse nelle sue opere.

Anche Soane come tanti altri architetti inglesi fece un viaggio di studio in Italia, non solo per osservare un dato numero di monumenti ma anche per familiarizzarsi con il tipo di studi dei vincitori del Gran Prix francese. Essendo uno degli architetti piú avanzati stilisticamente di quel periodo, Soane progettó parecchi progetti visionari di stile neoclassico, ma la sua continua pre-occupazione con quel tipo di opera lo pose in una posizione distaccata dagli altri, come nel caso del ponte trionfale (un progetto standard del Gran Prix) al quale ritornó spesso come ispirazione negli anni seguenti. Soane é chiaramente indebitato ai romanticisti del classicismo francese specialmente Le Camus de Mezières e E. L. Boullée. La sua ambizione di riuscire a formulare uno stile personale che lo staccasse dai suoi contemporanei é parzialmente dovuta alla sua conoscenza della teoria francese ed al suo interesse nella vera struttura della cattedrale Gotica e di altri edifici pubblici.

La profonda influenza di Laugier, che aveva arricchito con le sue dottrine riduttive i suoi saggi su Palladio scelti per la publicazione nel suo libro *Plans, Elevations and Sections*, del 1788, riappare nelle conferenze di Soane date alla Royal Academy dal 1809 in poi. Non solo Soane condanna gli elementi antifunzionali conformandosi ai principi di Laugier contro l'ornamento, e quindi censura alcune delle sue opere migliori, ma anche si allontana dalle dottrine di Chambers i cui *Treatise* vedevano gli ordini come elementi principalmente decorativi.

Oltre a George Dance c'erano altri architetti la cui opera seguiva la stessa direzione di Soane, Thomas Leverton, John Tasker e S. P. Cockerell in Inghilterra, e Benjamin Latrobe in America, specialmente nelle camere interne del Campidoglio a Washington D.C. Il famoso contemporaneo di Soane John Nash gli era marginalmente vicino come esponente dello stile pittoresco, ma radicalmente diverso in tutti i fatti fondamentali. Nash aveva usato un sistema di lucernai a Buckingham Palace simile a quello usato da Soane nelle gallerie di casa sua.

Lo smembramento della forma architectonica di Soane in spazi scavati e illuminati ha qualche somiglianza con la tarda opera del pittore J. M. W. Turner, suo caro amico, perché ambedue erano interassati nell'uso della luce. La rappresentazione pittorica dell'architettura attraverso dipinti ad acquerello, che era stato tracciata da Turner, era una naturale derivazione della sensibilità pittoresca. Le illustrazioni degli *Sketches in Architecture* (1793) e i grandi acquerelli prodotti nel suo studio in quel periodo sono molto vicini all'opera di Turner. Soane collaboró con Turner, quando quest' ultimo era professore di prospettiva alla Royal Academy, nella preparazione di disegni illustrativi, ed é chiaro dalle correzioni fatte da Soane che Turner non solo era preoccupato dagli effetti della luce nella pittura ma anche, come Soane, era interessato nella corretta esposizione di dipinti. L'influenza di Soane su Turner si manifesta nel progetto di una casa con galleria in uno stile Italianesco costruita per il pittore nel 1819–21.

Rassomiglianze con l'opera di Soane possono essere trovate nei, progetti di altri architetti inglesi: John Foulson (1772–1842), James Spiller (1760–1829), David Laing (1774–1856), Thomas Harrison (1774–1829), John Dobson (1787–1865), Sir Jeffrey Wyatville (1760–1840) e W. J. Donthorn (1799–1859). In Europa si possono trovare delle somiglianze tra Soane e lo stile Franco-Prussiano attorno al 1800, nell'opera di architetti come Gilly minore e maggiore, Gentz e Weinbrenner. Anche se Schinkel é della generazione successiva a Soane, vi sono varie somiglianze tra i due nell'evoluzione delle rispettive carriere e nel suo modo di usare la forma architettonica per produrre effetti lineari e astringenti, o pittoreschi e poetici.

Watkin conclude citando una serie di testi contemporanei che illustrano il tipo di critica al quale Soane era stato sottoposto durante la sua vita sottolineando il suo isolamento dai suoi contemporanei con i quali aveva cosi poco in comune.

G.-Tilman Mellinghoff nel suo articolo 'La Galleria di Dulwich Rivisitata' riassume la storia dell'edificio e descrive il processo di progettazione che Soane seguí nel creare un monumento unico per il suo caro amico Sir Francis Bourgeois, che aveva donato 360 dipinti per il collegio. La galleria di Dulwich fu progettata da Soane nel 1811 nel periodo migliore della sua vita, quando aveva giá formato il suo stile introverso, ed é considerata da molti come il suo piu grande successo. Era un opera che gli stava molto a cuore poiché le aveva dedicato speciale personali energie come é confermato dalla quantitá, varietá, e inconsistenza delle piante che ancora rimangono a testimoniare l'importanza che quel lavoro ebbe per lui.

L'intenzione di Bourgeois era di costruire un mausoleo di marmo simile a quello che Soane aveva progettato per il suo compagno Noel Desenfans, il fondatore di questa collezione. I dipinti sarebbero dovuti essere appesi nella galleria del vecchio collegio propriamente riadattato e restaurato. Soane chiaramente intendeva ricostruire il complesso fin dall'inizio e le prime cinque proposte che furono presentate nel maggio 1811 disponevano gli edifici a forma di quadrilatero e la vecchia cappella veniva conservata. Benché questi progetti furono respinti per tutto il periodo delle guerre napoleoniche, Soane non abbandono mai l'idea, in tutti i progetti successivi, di concepire la galleria come un futuro quadrilatero.

Da questa idea del quadrangolo si sviluppo lentamente il progetto della galleria. Nelle primi soluzioni appaiano due diverse varianti stilistiche che formano un'armoniosa composizione con la cappella esistente: ambedue formano una tensione tra gli elementi classici e gotici, ma nessuna delle due soluzioni é veramente felice. Dopo una serie di rielaborazioni nelle quali le piante vengono riorganizzate, emergono quelle finali. Sono molto piú spoglie e richiedono una maggiore manipolazione stilistica prima di costituire la terza ed ultima fase della progettazione. La ricerca di una soluzione meno cara porta a una versione piú semplice, spoglia ma il cui classicismo, pur se drasticamente ridotto e riinterpretato, rimane sorprendente. Persino dopo che la prima pietra fu posata nell'ottobre 1811 ci fu un importante cambiamento: il mausoleo fu mosso dalla facciata est a quella ovest creando un diverso accento. La costruzione andó avanti rapidamente e l'involucro dell'edificio fu finito verso la metá del 1813 i dipinti arrivarono nel 1814 e l'edificio innaugurato nel 1815.

Anche se c'é la tentazione di riferire la galleria di Dulwich ai progetti per musei dei Gran Prix francesi, esso ha molto di piú in comune con la tradizione inglese della galleria privata nella residenza di campagna, la cui evoluzione architettonica comincia con l'allontanamento della lunga galleria. Soane nel suo progetto de 1787 per una galleria a Fonthill House trova necessario dividere la lunga galleria tradizionale, ma a Dulwich viene trasformata in una sistemazione per una serie di sale per esposizione. É qui che avviene il salto dall'osservazione privata a quella pubblica. Qualche galleria importante era gia stata costruita prima di Dulwich, la galleria di Castle Howard di C. T. Tatham (1801–12) era la piú recente, ma Dulwich é l'unica nel suo genere poiché é la prima galleria che da una espressione esterna alla funzione interna.

Soane considerava il mausoleo la parte piú importante di Dulwich, il microcosmo della suprema percezione romantica, dell'idea di una morte transcendentale. La sua unione con la galleria fu un'idea di Soane come nel caso Gilly, forse é stata inspirata dal costume medievale di seppellire il fondatore di una chiesa nella chiesa stessa. L'effetto del mausoleo é accentuato da un leggero decoro di stile greco con uno spazio di tipo bizantino. Una lanterna nascosta emette una quieta luce ambrata nella camera funebre e crea quella 'lumière mystérieuse' delle chiese Francesi tanto ammirata da Soane.

Il lucernaio veniva usato, a quel tempo, a Londra solo nei saloni delle aste e nelle gallerie per via della loro necessità di superfici murali, ma l'arrivo della galleria Fonthill di Soane, lo rese il metodo di illuminazione piu usato, come testimoniano le gallerie di Petworth, Panshanger, Brocklesby é Attingham. L'illuminazione e l'architettura furono criticate sia in quel periodo che piú tardi. Siccome la galleria di Dulwich pone incertezza sulla validità delle regole classiche é chiaro che irritava e confondeva i contemporanei di Soane.

Varie aggiunte nell'ottocento e novecento hanno allargato l'edificio da una serie di cinque sale a una costruzione con tre file di quattordici stanze.

Per concludere, Dulwich non é soltanto un'altra opera di Soane, ma é la sua preferita e per la quale non chiese di essere pagato ed era persino disposto a pagare di tasca sua quando ci furono problemi finanziari. Per Soane rappresentó una sfida in cui la sua amicizia con Bourgeois trovó modo di espressione in un ideale scenario pastorale. Dulwich fu il risultato di un lento e preciso processo, con vari stadi di progettazione, e cambió da un progetto senza pretese ad una delle piú individuali espressioni dell'architettura di Soane, considerata da molti come il culmine della sua architettura.

Resumen en español

Sir John Summerson en su estudio 'Soane: el hombre y el estilo', versión revisada y reelaborada de su libro *Sir John Soane* (1952), identifica los elementos característicos del estilo Soane en dos formas; primero observando el aspecto general de la carrera del arquitecto y segundo su vida profesional durante sus años de formación. El estilo Soane es una de las curiosidades de la arquitectura Europea y hacia el año 1790 cuando este empezó a madurar, no existía ningún otro arquitecto en Europa que estuviera tan poco atado por la lealtad hacia lo clásico, tan libre en el manejo de las proporciones y tan aventurado en el uso de las estructuras y de la iluminación como Soane demostró estar al construir entonces el Banco de Inglaterra.

La carrera de Soane se divide en cinco períodos: El período de estudiante entre 1776–1780 (de los 23 a los 27 años) en los que Soane estaba influenciado mayormente por el Neoclasicismo francés; el primer período de práctica de 1780 a 1791 (27–38) durante el que construyó, más que nada, casas de campo en las que se advierte la influencia de Wyatt y de Holland. El período Intermedio, entre 1791 y 1806, es considerado el más creativo de su carrera durante el que trabajó en diversos estudios de arquitectura y es entonces cuando surgen los elementos característicos del estilo Soane. Durante el período que abarca de 1806 a 1821 (de los 53 a los 68 años) Soane atraviesa una época problemática en su vida personal y es aquí cuando los diferentes elementos de su estilo se combinan de formas diversas obteniendo nuevos efectos pintorescos a los cuales el mismo denomina 'poesia de la Arquitectura'. En su último período de 1821 a 1833 (68–80 años de edad) Soane proyecta en solitario grandes edificios públicos enfrentándose a la crítica, y después de esto, vuelve al Neoclasicismo.

Summerson dirige su atención hacia un número de temas individuales pertenecientes al período Intermedio, el período mas creativo de Soane, y demuestra como se desarrolló y expandió más tarde en el período Pintoresco. Esta época incluye la cúpula colgante y el 'óculo', ventanas semicirculares sobre segmentos de arco, el techo de bóveda cruzada y la sustitución de un orden clásico por lineas de pilastras, claro síntoma del primitivismo de Laugier al cual Soane se suscribió.

Es entre los 38 y los 45 años cuando Soane completa el rápido desarrollo de su estilo y hasta entonces ninguno de sus trabajos habia sido ni derivativo ni sin éxito. Durante su período Pintoresco, llamado así porque su trabajo es análogo al de los paisajistas y teóricos de la escuela Pintoresca, los temas existentes eran recombinados y reinterpretados sin que ningun tema nuevo fuera añadido. Fue tambien durante este tiempo cuando Soane llegó a concebir su propio estilo como unificador de potencialidades no solo concernientes a diferentes tipos de clasicismo sino tambien de estilo gótico.

No cabe duda de que Soane tiene una gran influencia de George Dance, para quien trabajó en sus primeros años de profesion y en ciertas ocasiones existen documentos y pequeños apuntes explanatorios hechos por el mismo Dance y que prueban su colaboración con Soane en casos como el del 'Bank Stock Office' (la Bolsa). No se pretende en forma alguna sugerir que la arquitectura de Soane haya sido hecha por Dance, ya que ambos son muy diferentes y Soane tenía un temperamento inconfundible. Pero de lo que no existe duda es de que el estilo Soane es el producto no de un solo hombre, sino de dos, y Soane nunca dejó de reconocer su deuda hacia Dance.

Summerson concluye su estudio con una mirada a los últimos años dc Soane, despues de haberse retirado de la vida profesional en 1833 a la edad de 80 años. En ese mismo año Soane recibió el Acta Privada del Parlamento bajo la cual, su casa y lo en ella contenido se convertian en Institución Nacional despues de su muerte. Esta decisión significó para Soane el final de un sueño en el que un dia él seria sucedido por un hijo tambien arquitecto, un ideal dinástico querido de tal forma que llevó a su hijo a sublevarse contra él. El museo continuó aumentando sus objetos hasta el dia de su muerte en 1837, con la notable adquisición delas pinturas de la 'Eleccion' de Hogarth y del sarcofago Belzoni y se mantienen hoy en dia en memoria suya sirviendo a la profesión que amó con tan feroz pasión.

El artículo de David Watkin 'Soane y sus contemporáneos' se refiere a las similitudes y diferencias entre el trabajo de Soane y el de sus contemporáneos tanto en su propio país como en el extranjero. El caso de Soane nos presenta la paradoja del arquitecto envuelto en la tradicion clásica y que, al mismo tiempo, es un artista romántico, siguiendo un camino solitario en un estilo idiosincrático; su trabajo demuestra su agudeza visual e intelectual derivada de la fructífera tensión entre la doctrina pública y la práctica privada. Estudiar a Soane es encontrarse de frente con el problema de la espresión de la propia personalidad en arquitectura, ya que es posible encontrar en su trabajo claros reflejos de las cualidades sobresalientes de su carácter.

Como muchos otros arquitectos ingleses, también Soane emprendió un largo viaje de estudios por Italia, experiencia que envolvia, no solo el estudio de una larga lista de monumentos, sino también el familiarizarse con los ganadores del 'Grand Prix' francés.

Así como los arquitectos más avanzados de la época, Soane también proyecto una serie de imágenes neoclásicas visionarias, pero su continua preocupación por ellos le apartó un tanto de su tiempo, como sucede en el caso del proyecto para un puente Triunfal (tipico ejemplo del 'Grand Prix') al cual Soane volvió repetidamente durante los años. Soane tenia claramente una deuda con los románticos de la tradición clásica francesa, particularmente Le Camus de Mezières y E.L. Boullée. El ímpetu de conseguir una manera de proyectar tan personal que le apartara de sus contemporáneos parece derivar, en parte, de su conocimiento de las teorías francesas y en parte de su interés en la verdadera estructura gótica de las catedrales y de otros edificios públicos.

La profunda influencia de Laugier, cuyas doctrinas reduccionistas habián avivado los elegantes escritos Paladianos elegidos para ser publicados en 1788 en su libro *Plans, Elevations and Sections*; reaparecen en las conferencias dadas por Soane en la Real Academia de 1809 en adelante. No sólo se condenaban en ellas los elementos antifuncionales de acuerdo con los principios anti-ornamentales de Laugier, lo que implica que, por lo tanto, censuraba algunos de sus propios y mas elegantes interiores, sino que tambien se disociaba de las doctrinas de Chambers cuyo *Treatise* consideraba los órdenes clásicos como mayormente decorativos.

Aparte de los trabajos de George Dance, evidencias de otros arquitectos que siguieron líneas similares a la de Soane, se pueden apreciar en los trabajos de Thomas Leverton, John Tasker y S.P. Cockerell en Inglaterra y Benjamin Latrobe en America, este último especialmente en su diseño de interiores para el edificio Capitol de Washington, de clara influencia Soane. John Nash, su famoso contemporáneo, difiere de éste claramente en todo lo fundamental y está solo superficialmente cercano al exponente de lo pintoresco. Nash empleó un sistema de iluminación cenital similar al empleado por Soane en las galerías de su propia casa y en Buckingham Palace.

Soane presenta una disolución de la forma arquitectural en espacios poéticamente iluminados y como 'excavados' de una totalidad lo que resembla claramente el trabajo de su amigo el pintor J.M. Turner, ambos artistas presentan similar preocupacion por el tema de la luz.

La representación pictórica de la arquitectura a través de seductoras acuarelas, de las cuales Turner era un pionero, era un producto de la pintoresca sensibilidad de Soane y tanto sus *Sketches in Architecture* (1793) como las enormes acuarelas producidas para representar los proyectos durante aquel tiempo, están muy relacionadas con el trabajo de Turner. Soane colaboró con él en la preparación de unos dibujos de demostración cuando éste último fué nombrado profesor de perspectiva en la 'Real Academia'; y se observa claramente en las modificaciones introducidas entonces que la gran preocupación de Turner por la luz iba acompañada de un cuidado extremado en la apropiada disposición de los cuadros, preocupación que compartía con Soane. La influencia de Turner sobre Soane queda de manifiesto en el proyecto para una casa 'Italiana' y una galería de cuadros, construidas ambas para si mismo en 1819–21.

Paralelismos con el trabajo de Soane se pueden encontrar en arquitectos ingleses como John Foulson (1772–1842), James Spiller (1760–1829), David Laing (1774–1856), Thomas Harrison (1774–1829), John Dobson (1787–1865), Sir Jeffrey Wyatville (1766–1840) y W.J. Donthorn (1789–1859). En el resto de Europa se pueden encontrar ciertas afinidades entre Soane y el estilo Franco-Prusiano de los alrededores de 1800, en los trabajos de arquitectos como Gilly, Gentz y Weinbrenner. Schinkel, aunque perteneciente a una generación más joven que Soane, coincide con él en la forma en que su carrera se desarrolló y también en el manejo de la forma arquitectónica para producir ciertos efectos de tipo lineal y astringentes o, por el contrario, pintorescos y poéticos.

En resumen, Watkin comenta acerca de una gran variedad de escritos de entonces la crítica de que el artista fué objeto durante su vida, enfatizando su aislamiento de sus contemporáneos con los que tenia tan poco en común.

G-Tilman Mellinghoff, en su articulo 'Una segunda visita a la Pinacoteca de Dulwich' provee una imagen condensada de la historia del edificio y aclara el complejo proceso de diseño a través del cual Soane creó un monumento único para su querido amigo Sir P. Bourgeois y su legado de 360 cuadros al colegio de Dulwich. La Pinacoteca fue proyectada por Soane en 1811 cuando se encontraba en el mayor apogeo de su vida profesional y habiá adquirido ya su propio estilo. El edificio está considerado por muchos especialistas como su mayor éxito, fué una de las obras mas queridas de Soane y a la que dedicó gran energia personal como se comprueba en la enorme variedad, cantidad e inconsistencia de los planos que se conservan.

La idea original de Bourgeois habia sido el construir un mausoleo de mármol que fuera, en mayor o menor grado, una copia del construido por Soane para su compañero Noel Desenfans, promotor de la coleccion que habiá de encerrar el museo adecuadamente adaptado y reparado. Reconstruir el edificio era claramente la intención inicial de Soane y los cinco primeros diseños entregados en Mayo de 1811 eran para un nuevo edificio cuadrangular en el que se conservaba la capilla original. Aunque no fué aceptado durante el período de las guerras Napoleónicas, era muy característico de Soane el no olvidar una idea y en todos los proyectos que siguieron al primero se explica el museo o galería como parte de un edificio cuadrangular.

La galería se desarrolló a partir de esta idea del cuadrado. En el primen proyecto aparecen dos versiones estilísticas diferentes, ambas como parte de un esfuerzo por crear una armoniosa conjunción con la capilla existente, ambas en tension entre elementos clásicos y góticos, aún asi, ninguna fue un auténtico éxito. Siguiendo una serie de escritos en los que las plantas se reorganizaban, los planos finales surgieron con un diseño mucho más sencillo y requiriendo una remodelación estilística substancial que constituyó la tercera y última fase del proceso. Fue la búsqueda de una solución menos costosa la que condujo el cambio hacia una versión más sencilla en la que destaca claramente su afirmación de temas clasicistas drásticamente simplificados.

Incluso cuando la construcción de los cimientos de piedra se hallaba ya terminada en Octubre de 1811 se sucede un gran cambio en el proyecto al decidir trasladar el mausoleo del frente Este al frente Oeste, creando, por consiguiente, efectos diferentes de los calculados. La construcción progresaba rapidamente y el esqueleto de la galería se termino a mediados de 1813, los cuadros llegaban en 1814 y fue inaugurada en 1815.

Aunque existe la tentación de relacionar la galería de Dulwich con los diseños del 'Grand Prix' francés para museos, es un proyecto que tiene mas puntos en común con la tradición inglesa de la galería de pinturas en la casa de campo privada. Soane decidió en su propio proyecto para una galería en Fonthill House, en 1787, dividir el tipo tradicional de galería, pero es al proyectar Dulwich cuando se produce el cambio vital con la transición entre la exposición al público y la privada. Un gran número de galerías importantes habia sido construido antes que Dulwich de la cuales 'Castle Howard Gallery' de C.H. Tatham (1801–1812) era la mas parecida, pero la diferencia entre Dulwich y cualquiera de sus predecesoras era que Dulwich fue la primera en dar expresión externa a la función interna y, como tal, es única.

El mausoleo fue considerado por Soane como la parte mas importante de Dulwich, un microcosmo del todo y una sublime realización de la idea del romanticismo acerca de la muerte trascendental. La combinación de galería y mausoleo fue una idea original de Soane y tal como en el caso de Gilly podria haber estado inspirada en la costumbre medieval de situar en las iglesias la tumba de su fundador. El efecto del mausoleo es producto de la sutileza de la decoración griega y de la atmósfera bizantina; una linterna semiescondida, dando una luz apagada en la cámara del sarcófago para crear el efecto misterioso que Soane tanto admiraba en las iglesias francesas.

El sistema de iluminación cenital era entonces usado en Londres en salas de exposiciones y subastas debido a la gran necesidad de paredes libres para tales ocasiones; pero el impacto causado por la galería Fonthill creado por Soane convirtió este modo de iluminación en la moda preferida como queda patente en las galerías Petworth, Panshanger, Brockleby y Attingham. Tanto el sistema de iluminación como la arquitectura misma fueron objeto de una dura crítica tanto entonces como mas adelante.

Era de esperar que Dulwich confundiera a sus contemporáneos ya que ponía en duda la validez de las reglas clásicas. Una serie de extensiones durante los siglos 19 y 20 transformaron el edificio desde una serie de 5 habitaciones a todo un complejo de 14 habitaciones dispuestas en tres hileras.

En resumen Dulwich no era uno de los proyectos mas corrientes de Soane sino uno de los mas personales por el que no cobró honorarios y por el que estaba dispuesto a pagar en caso de que surgieran dificultades económicas. Fue para él un desafío a través del cual, su amistad con Bourgeois encontró expresión en el escenario rural ideal. Dulwich era el resultado de un lento y doloroso proceso con muchas fases de diseño y surgió de una idea sin pretensiones como una de las expresiones mas individuales en la arquitectura de Soane y considerada por muchos como el mayor de sus logros.